WITH

HEART

AND

MIND

AND

Soul

WITH
HEART
AND
MIND
AND
Soul

A Guide to Prayer For
College Students and Young Adults

Helen R. Neinast
Thomas C. Ettinger

UPPER
ROOM BOOKS

WITH HEART AND MIND AND SOUL:
A Guide to Prayer for College Students and Young Adults

Copyright © 1994 by Helen R. Neinast and Thomas C. Ettinger
All rights reserved.

The publisher gratefully acknowledges permission to reproduce the copyrighted material appearing in this book. Credit lines for this material appear on page 235 and following.

Scripture quotations not otherwise identified are from the New Revised Standard Version of the Bible, copyright 1989 by the Division of Christian Education of the National Council of the Churches of Christ in the United States of America, and are used by permission.

Scripture quotations designated NIV are from the *Holy Bible, New International Version.* Copyright © 1973, 1978, 1984 International Bible Society. Used by permission of Zondervan Bible Publishers.

Cover illustration and design: Bret Haines
First Printing: May 1994 (7)
ISBN 0-8358-0695-2
Library of Congress Catalog Card Number: 93-61047

Printed in the United States of America

CONTENTS

WITH

HEART

AND

MIND

AND

Soul

ও
INTRODUCTION

'MY OWN HIGH SCHOOL AND COLLEGE YEARS WERE A MIXTURE of joy and pain."

That's the way Madeleine L'Engle, well-known author of books for children and adults, sums up her experiences in higher education. In *Two-Part Invention: The Story of a Marriage*, she goes on to describe some of the wondrous—as well as some of the more distressing—things that happened to her in college.

For most of you—whether you're in a job just after high school, in your first year of college, starting your senior year, or heading into graduate school—L'Engle's description of life in these years is probably strikingly real. There are times of great joy and discovery ahead for you. And, most likely, times of struggle and challenge await you as well.

Early in his public ministry, Jesus was asked what thought was the core of the Christian faith. He responded by urging believers to love God with their whole being—"with all your heart, and with all your soul, and with all your mind"—and to love their neighbors as themselves (Matt. 22:37). It is with this biblical understanding that we approach the spiritual life.

This book, *WITH HEART AND MIND AND SOUL*, is meant to be a companion for you along your way—both in good times and bad. It can be a help to you in strengthening your relationship with God. Use it as a guide to develop a spiritual discipline of prayer and reflection that will support you in your growth as a Christian and as a student.

WHAT TO DO WITH THIS BOOK

Use this book either by yourself or with a study group. If you are using it on your own, you may want to start with Week 1 and work your way straight through to Week 36. Or, as you look through the Contents pages, you may find one particular subject that speaks directly to an immediate concern of yours. In that case, go to that chapter and use it for a week.

If you are part of a study group using this book, you and members of the group should agree on which chapter to use each week. Again, it doesn't matter whether you work your way straight through the book or skip around, as long as everyone in the group is clear on the chapter designated for study in the coming week.

Whether on your own or in a study group, the daily discipline is the same.

OPENING PRAYER AND SCRIPTURE FOCUS. Each week's reflection begins with a prayer calling you to be mindful of God's presence. This marks the beginning of your devotional time. There is also a Scripture Focus for each week. The Opening Prayer and Scripture Focus are a good way for you to "center down" for study and reflection.

Start by praying the Opening Prayer. Then read the Scripture Focus, either silently or aloud. Give yourself some time to sit in silence. Allow the silence to quiet your mind and heart. Open yourself to hear what God has to say to you.

DAILY SCRIPTURE READINGS. The Daily Scripture Readings are chosen to add to and expand the theme for reflection each week. Find a translation of the Bible that speaks to you, and use it to read each day's scripture.

The Bible is our best source for exploring who God is and who God calls us to be. The Gospels, in particular, reveal to us God's grace in Jesus, available to everyone. The Gospels set us on a course to read, understand, and learn what it means to be followers of Christ.

As you read each scripture, ask yourself several questions: What does the scripture have to say about the week's theme? How does that scripture apply to your life? How does it apply to what is going on in the world? Open yourself to hear what the scriptures have to say to you each day.

FOCUS FOR REFLECTION. ˙After you have read the scripture for the day, read the Focus for Reflection. The focus may be on some specific issue in your life—decision-making, grades, money—or it may deal with some part of your spiritual life—prayer, Bible study, forgiveness.

As you read the Focus for Reflection, make notes about any feelings or questions the piece raises for you.

POINTS OF DEPARTURE. Following the Focus for Reflection are writings collected from different sources. Some are poetry, some are song lyrics, some are by writers who lived centuries ago, some are from contemporary persons. Use these writings as points of departure for your own reflection on the week's theme. Read them each day, and let yourself be guided to the one that calls to you most strongly that day. Again, as with the Focus for Reflection, make notes about any feelings or questions the Points of Departure raise for you.

Because we are sensitive to inclusive language about people (not using only *he* when the pronoun actually includes both men and women) and inclusive language for God, we have changed male generic language to inclusive language wherever possible. In places where copyright holders did not give us permission to make changes, we left the original wording. As you read, keep in mind that these authors were often writing without an understanding of our more recent concerns about inclusive language.

JOURNALING: IDEAS FOR WRITTEN REFLECTION. Don't be intimidated by this section. "Journaling" is really nothing more than keeping track of what's going on inside you as you read and reflect. You may already be in the habit of journal keeping. You may have never kept a journal in your life. It doesn't matter. Now is a good time to begin—or to continue—keeping a journal.

In her article "Journaling: Breathing Space in the Spiritual Journey," Jan Johnson says that a spiritual journal tries to answer the question "What is God doing in my life?" Such a journal gives you a place to begin "to identify and evaluate the pattern" of your relationship with God.

In this kind of journal keeping, God is the only one with whom you need share what you write. Your journal should be a safe place where you can record your feelings, your fears, your insights, and your questions.

You can use the ample space provided in this book to write, or you may want to buy a notebook. If you use a separate notebook for writing, keep your journal with this book. Use the journal suggestions each week to explore your thoughts, reactions, and feelings about what you read in this book and in the scripture passages. If you're not sure what your feelings are, remember that confusion is a feeling, too. Just put pen to paper and see what happens. Let your journal help you to linger over your reflection and prayer time.

Try to write every day. Some days you may have a lot to write; other days, you may write only one or two sentences. That doesn't matter. What matters is that you keep writing. Keeping a spiritual journal over a few months or a year gives you a chance to look back at where you have been and to look forward to where you are going in your spiritual life. As you keep your journal, read through it often to see what patterns and changes mark your spiritual journey. This can be a great way to learn more about yourself and about how God is working in your life.

PRAYERS. At the end of each chapter are prayer suggestions for the world, for others, and for yourself. Use them to focus, to center, and to begin your prayer time. You might list at the end of each journal entry your specific prayer concerns for that day or week.

Be honest in your prayers to God. Express your gratitude, make your confession, be straightforward about your doubts, share *all* your feelings. Talk to God from your heart.

Then, take time to listen. Sit quietly to hear what God has to say to you. Listen for words of challenge from God as well as words of comfort. Rest in the peace God offers you, and rejoice in the strength God brings you.

FINDING A QUIET TIME AND PLACE

Finding the right time and place for your prayer and meditation is a very personal thing. Some people function best in the mornings; others find their quiet time at the end of the day. It may take you a while to discover what time works best for you. Experiment until something feels right.

Whether you choose morning, noon, mid-afternoon, or the end of the day, the important thing is to develop a pattern, some regular time and place set aside for daily prayer and meditation. Choose a quiet place and a time with relatively few distractions. Then, keep your appointment with God at that time and in that place each day.

Some people find that lighting a candle or sitting quietly for a few moments and breathing deeply helps them to focus their prayer time. Listen to your own inner spirit, and let yourself be guided as you discover ways to begin and end your quiet time with God.

What if you miss a day? This will surely happen. Don't be compulsive about it, and don't berate yourself. God wants you to grow in grace, not set yourself up for failure. The spiritual life is one of gradual growth, not perfectionism. God does not expect perfection from you; maybe you shouldn't expect it from yourself, either.

USING THIS BOOK WITH A GROUP

If you are in a study group that is using this book, you have made an important commitment to yourself and to group members. You are making a covenant with yourself to make time for prayer and reflection daily; you are making a covenant with the group to meet weekly for community prayer and reflection.

There will, of course, be occasions when you miss your daily prayer and reflection time, or a week when you're not able to make the group meeting. That will happen. Don't criticize yourself too harshly—you made a commitment to be faithful to your discipline, not to be compulsive about it. Just get back on track as soon as you can.

Your group will need to decide on a regular meeting place and time. Early morning, before classes start, might be best for your group. Noon time, with each person bringing a brown bag lunch, might work. Early evening with a snack supper together before the meeting might work best. Late at night, just after the library closes, might also be a possibility.

As mentioned earlier, the group will need to agree on the order in which to study the chapters in the book so that everyone will know which chapter is designated for each week. Allow about one hour for the group meeting. Your group may choose to have a formal "leader" throughout the study, or it may decide to share leadership, with each group member taking the lead a week at a time.

Begin each session by praying together the Opening Prayer for the past week's study. After the prayer, experience some silent time as a group. Use this time to quiet body and mind, to leave behind whatever activities you've just come from, to center yourselves.

Close the silent prayer time by reading aloud the Scripture Focus. After this, check in with each group member. What was the week's experience like for them? Was it easy or hard to keep up with the Daily Scripture Readings, prayer, and journal time? Were people able to get into a rhythm of prayer and study this week? If so, what did that feel like? If not, what are some of the reasons?

What was the actual experience of prayer like this week for different group members? Was it full and rich, or were there some "dry" days? As people share the ups and downs of their spiritual life, be supportive. If a group member mentions a problem that you have been having, share your experience also. If someone asks for suggestions or help, listen carefully and contribute any ideas you might have.

It is important to accept whatever group members say about their week's experiences and efforts with openness and compassion. Don't be judgmental. But don't be afraid to give caring feedback, either.

Next, move to a group discussion of the Daily Scripture Readings. At this point persons may share which scriptures meant the most to them. Which ones troubled or challenged members of the group? In what ways? Which ones were comforting or reassuring? Why? Persons may read aloud any of the scriptures they found particularly powerful.

Look at the Focus for Reflection and the Points of Departure together. Share reactions to these. What questions or feelings did these raise for group members? What insights came through the readings? Did some particular reading speak in a special way to different members of the group?

Now, go through the journaling questions. Encourage one another to be honest and open in this discussion. Some may want to read parts of their journal entries for the rest of the group. Don't pressure anyone to read from her or his journal; these reflections are part of a very private conversation between the individual and God. But if some want to share part of their journal, accept their offering with care, respect, and confidentiality.

Finally, share with one another any prayer requests, celebrations, or concerns that came up during the week. Persons should list these in their journals, so that they can remember them in prayer during the week ahead. Close with group prayer. There are several ways to do this. One person can begin the prayer by lifting up each of the concerns and celebrations mentioned before, pausing for a moment after each one. Then, spend time in shared silence, and end the prayer with everyone praying the Lord's Prayer.

The group may use a circle form of prayer with everyone joining hands. One person will begin the prayer; when finished, he or she will squeeze the hand of the person either to the right or left. This person may then either pray aloud or pass the prayer on to the next person with a squeeze of the hand. Continue until the prayer goes completely around the circle.

KEEP AT IT

Whether you are using this book alone or with a group, the most important thing to remember about developing and growing in a spiritual discipline of reflection and prayer is this: Keep at it, no matter what. There will be times when you will find it easy to keep your daily commitment to God and to yourself. There will be other times when you find it next to impossible to quiet yourself for prayer and reflection.

Sometimes you'll be eager to pick up the Bible and read. Other times, you will hardly remember what you read.

Some days you'll find yourself caught up in the power of the presence of God; other days you will feel as though you're simply going through the motions. It doesn't matter. Just keep at it. You will be surprised at the changes God can work in your life in the weeks and months ahead when you come to God with heart and mind and soul.

1

FINDING A SPIRITUAL HOME

Opening Prayer

God, you know me. You know what I need. Help me to seek and find a community in which I may grow closer to you. Amen.

Scripture Focus

The word of God continued to spread; the number of disciples increased greatly. (Acts 6:7)

Daily Scripture Readings

Sunday	Psalm 122
Monday	Acts 2:43-47
Tuesday	Matthew 18:20
Wednesday	Romans 1:8-12
Thursday	Matthew 7:24-27
Friday	Philippians 1:3-11
Saturday	1 Peter 3:8-16

The Focus for Reflection

A HURRICANE HAD JUST MADE ITS SWEEP THROUGH Tallahassee, complete with 100-mile-per-hour winds, damaged homes, and downed power lines. At 3:00 A.M. my phone rang. I answered it sleepily, surprised that phone service had been restored so soon.

The caller was a student from the campus. He said that he had decided to kill himself and was about to follow through. But he was scared. He was shocked at how far he had taken things, and he was calling to see if I would come to talk with him.

The ten-mile drive to the United Methodist campus ministry center at Florida State University took an unusually long time as my little MGB negotiated fallen trees, downed utility poles and power lines.

I finally reached my office; the student was waiting for me. Feeling the stress of the hazardous drive and realizing the pressure of the moment, I looked at the student and said, "This had better be good, or I'll kill you myself!"

That broke the tension, and we laughed. In fact, as the hours and the early morning conversation unfolded, we found ourselves laughing *and* crying, making plans together. I asked for and got from him a promise not to commit suicide during the next four months, and in return I promised him we would spend that time working together to discover if he could find reason enough to want to live.

In the weeks that followed, as our conversations continued and as he became more involved in the campus ministry community, he took a close look at himself. He discovered much, changed many things about himself (for he was in reality a very courageous young man), and, through the care of other Christians, began to experience the depth of God's love for him.

He had found in that particular Christian community at Florida State a spiritual home. In the middle of his pain, he came to realize the importance of the fellowship and witness of other Christians in his life. During our four-month commitment to one another, he and I came to understand some of what goes into the making of a spiritual home that is healing, challenging, and supportive.

A true spiritual home is a community that accepts you as you are and encourages you to grow in faith. It provides avenues for Bible study that affirm Christ's redemptive power in your life. It allows you to have doubts, and it encourages you to talk about those doubts.

A spiritual home encourages you to use your reason and your experience to discover what the faith is all about. It challenges you to grow spiritually by reaching beyond yourself to others. Instead of providing easy answers, a spiritual home encourages prayer and reflection.

A spiritual home comforts you in your times of need and in turn needs you to comfort others. It loves you into loving others, even your enemies. It stands as a witness against racism, sexism, and prejudice, and it strengthens you to do the same.

A spiritual home basically helps you to discover God's will—God's deep yearning—for you and for your life.

That student? He is now the pastor of a church, helping to provide a spiritual home for himself and for others. He decided to live. Spiritual homes are just that important.

Points of Departure

♥ I told him that some people can create lives of holiness all by themselves, the way Mozart could create immortal music without taking piano lessons, but that most of us need a structure and the company of other people to do it.
—From *Who Needs God* by Harold Kushner

♥ You need the support and challenge of spiritual friends. Be open to finding such people. They are around, they come as gifts, and sooner or later grace will bring you together.
—From *The Awakened Heart* by Gerald G. May

♥ It is difficult to establish a rule of life to which one is faithful without the help of other similarly minded persons. A spiritual friend or a prayer group sharing similar values can be a great help in maintaining one's enthusiasm for growth in union with Christ.
—From *The Heart of the World* by Thomas Keating

♥ Going to church, even belonging to it, did not solve life's problems . . . but it gave me a sense of living in a larger context, of being part of something greater than what I could see through the tunnel vision of my personal concerns.
—From *Returning: A Spiritual Journey* by Dan Wakefield

♥ Your choice of a faith community is a crucial one for you to make. For if you are able to find a community that's right for you, there will be a fine rhythm of give and take between you and that community. It will help you lose yourself in a commitment and find yourself enabled and strengthened.
—From "Choosing a Community of Faith" by Sue Anne Steffey Morrow

♥ The Church is an "essential service" like the Post Office, but there will always be some narrow, irritating and inadequate officials behind the counter and you will always be tempted to exasperation by them.
—From *The Letters of Evelyn Underhill*

♥ If you are having difficulty deciding if a certain group is right for you, discuss the matter with someone whose judgment you trust; friends, relatives, professors, counselors, campus chaplains, residence hall and other staff members could offer advice.
—From "A Guide to Making Safe Judgments About Groups on Campus"

Journaling: Ideas for Reflection

As you search for a faith community, the place to begin is with yourself. Sue Anne Steffey Morrow, Associate Dean of the Chapel at Princeton University, suggests that you look at what your needs and desires are in relation to your faith. She asks several important questions. How important is worship to your faith life? What kind of worship—traditional, informal, experimental, is important to you? What about service to others?

Do you want to be stretched theologically, or do you need to be confirmed in your faith right now? Do you want to spend a big part of your social life with your faith community, or not? Take some time now to reflect and to think about what you want and need from a faith and fellowship group. Write your thoughts, questions, and discoveries in your journal.

What role can your commitment to a community of faith play in your education?

Prayers: For the World, for Others, for Myself

Spend a few moments in silence, asking God for guidance in getting involved with a faith community. Extend your prayers to all those who seek truth through the faith and through education. Pray for those who lead faith communities and for those who participate in them. Pray that those who are seeking a spiritual home may find one.

2
&

STUDY:
A Sacred Vocation

Opening Prayer
Creator of truth and wonder, lead my mind and heart in the search to understand, to invent, and to imagine. Amen.

Scripture Focus
Get wisdom; get insight. . . . (Proverbs 4:5)

Daily Scripture Readings

Sunday	Deuteronomy 4:5-8
Monday	1 Kings 4:29-34
Tuesday	Job 12:7-13
Wednesday	Psalm 119:33-40
Thursday	Proverbs 3:13-26
Friday	Mark 12:30
Saturday	Luke 2:41-52

The Focus for Reflection

IN HIS BOOK THE CENTERING MOMENT, HOWARD THURMAN has a wonderful prayer for the students of the world. He asks God to hold all students "steadily, quietly, with great concentration before Thy altar."

I came across this prayer during my first year in graduate school, and I kept a copy of it on my desk at home.

It wasn't until after several weeks of using this prayer each time I sat down to study that it occurred to me what Thurman must have meant by "Thy altar." Instead of seeing the traditional image of the altar in a church, I realized this prayer was calling me to consider my desk as God's altar—the altar upon which I made my daily offering of study.

That image brought me up short. To consider my studies as an offering to God gave new meaning and vitality to my work as a student. To be sure, there were days when my studies intrigued me, when the books I read inspired me and the papers I wrote felt insightful. But there were other days when my study was grudging, my mind dull, and my papers labored.

To use Thurman's image of my desk as an altar reminded me in a powerful way that all my study time—inspired or drudging, insightful or labored—belonged to God. It meant that, as I studied, I was blessing God. That prayer became for me a vivid reminder that my vocation as student was a sacred vocation.

As you approach your studies, remind yourself that God has called you at this time in your life to the vocation of student. As you approach your desk or your study carrel or the library, remind yourself that you are approaching God's altar. Offer your studies up to God, with thanksgiving for the gift of learning.

Points of Departure

♥ Quiet the mind before you seek the truth.
—From *Through the Labyrinth* by Peter Occhiogrosso

♥ There is divine beauty in learning, just as there is human beauty in tolerance. . . . To learn means to accept the postulate that life did not begin at my birth. Others have been here before me, and I walk in their footsteps.
—From "Have You Learned the Most Important Lesson of All?" by Elie Wiesel

♥ People don't realize how a man's [or woman's] whole life can be changed by *one* book.
—From *The Autobiography of Malcolm X*

♥ Some people fear ideas at least as much as nuclear bombs, and no wonder: ideas have tremendous power to shake and disrupt and make us uncomfortable.
—From *College: Getting in and Staying in* by D. Bruce Lockerbie and Donald R. Fonseca

♥ Too much concentration can be worse than none at all.
—From *God was in this Place and I, i Did Not Know* by Lawrence Kushner

♥ Facts, facts, facts . . . they are everywhere about me. . . . But facts are not the heart of my need. I need wisdom.
—From *Meditations of the Heart* by Howard Thurman

Journaling: Ideas for Reflection
John Belohlavek, a history professor at the University of South Florida, says that an active learner takes more risks than a passive one. He encourages taking intellectual risks in order to grow. How do you see yourself as a learner—active and involved, intimidated sometimes, stepping out into new arenas of thought? In what ways is time spent at your desk, in the classroom, or at the library "holy time"?

Prayers: For the World, for Others, for Myself

Consecrate your studies with prayer this week. Remind yourself of God's presence as you exercise your mind and intellect. Pray for students all around the world, in all places and circumstances of learning. Pray that their studies, and yours, bring about peace and healing in the world.

3

&

DISCIPLINE:
Spiritual and Otherwise

Opening Prayer

Help me to be faithful and fair in the discipline of my daily life, dear God. Amen.

Scripture Focus

And what does the Lord require of you but to do justice, and to love kindness, and to walk humbly with your God? (Micah 6:8*b*)

Daily Scripture Readings

Sunday	Psalm 34:4-10
Monday	Ephesians 6:18
Tuesday	Acts 1:6-11
Wednesday	1 Chronicles 16:11
Thursday	Colossians 1:9-14
Friday	Hebrews 12:1-13
Saturday	Luke 6:12

The Focus for Reflection

FOR SO MANY YEARS, IN SO MANY WAYS, I HAVE YEARNED TO BE close to you. Many of my followers have worked to help you understand that, to give you opportunities to be in fellowship with me. Parents, friends, pastors, teachers—at home, at play, in church, at school—through these and many others I have sought to send you a message: My love for you has no boundaries. I yearn to be with you.

I won't, however, force myself on you. The choice is yours. It is a choice you make through your own discipline now, for you are no longer a child relying on the faith of others.

The faith I offer challenges you, but it does not leave you to meet that challenge on your own. I have provided help and encouragement for even the weakest among you. Sit quietly for a moment and feel your deepest self-seeking peace. I will give you that peace. Listen.

I call you to a discipline of the spirit. As my Word says, you must be born again. For some of you, this may be a sudden movement of the spirit, the way Paul was struck on the road to Damascus. For most of you, your rebirth is a gradual journey stretching over the years. How you begin the journey does not matter. It matters only that you are on the way.

The discipline of the spirit responds to my touch through faithful prayer, study of scripture, fellowship with others, and outreach to those in need. A disciplined spirit has the courage to accept my loving forgiveness. If you cannot accept my forgiveness, you cannot forgive others. Nor can you learn to grow through your failings. To be whole, you must do both—and I yearn for you to be whole.

I call you to a discipline of the mind. Reach to learn. Seize each day with its opportunities to grow in intellect. Stretch your mind. Challenge yourself. I have given you the ability to learn that will last a lifetime. Use your ability, and sharpen those skills now. There are many ways in which your learning and study can contribute to the world's wholeness and healing. Discipline yourself with this gift, that you may be a blessing to others.

I also call you to a discipline of the heart. First, do no harm, but seek instead to understand those who are different from you. That understanding will open the storehouse of love I created inside you so that you may come to care not only for those who are different, but even for those you consider your enemies.

With a disciplined heart, you can better resist evil wherever you find it. I yearn for you to be watchful and responsive. The discipline of the heart is a call to stop the violence—economic, social, religious, and physical—that is inflicted on my children.

These disciplines are a challenge; and yet, I tell you that my yoke is easy and my burden light. For in the midst of it all—your joy and your laughter, your pain and your tears, your failings and your growth, your doubts and your fears—I will be with you. You will not be alone. Seek to trust me as a child, and I will lead you gently in the way.

Points of Departure

♥ There is a kind of nourishment our souls crave, even as our bodies need the right foods, sunshine, and exercise. Without that spiritual nourishment, our souls remain stunted and undeveloped.
—From *Who Needs God* by Harold Kushner

♥ When the mind is not agitated by many thoughts, it can settle down rather quickly into a synthesis of what one has been reading or thinking.
—From *The Heart of the World* by Thomas Keating

♥ The basic idea of meditation . . . is that it should make you more available to what is actually going on, and less caught up in your own preconceptions or emotional reactions to things.
—From *Through the Labyrinth* by Peter Occhiogrosso

♥ The more you seek for God, the nearer [God] will be to you.
—François Fénelon

♥ Sticking with something for a long period of time, the day in and day out of doing it, the living with it, was teaching me humility and patience I hadn't known before.
—From *Plain and Simple* by Sue Bender

Journaling: Ideas for Reflection

Consider the three disciplines of spirit, mind, and heart mentioned in the Focus for Reflection. Which of the three present the most challenges to you right now? Which is the hardest discipline to follow? Which is the easiest?

Someone once said that discipline is remembering what you want. Spend some time reflecting on what you want the life of your spirit, your mind, and your heart to look like. What daily disciplines do you need to observe in order to achieve what you want?

Prayers: For the World, for Others, for Myself
Pray for a discipline that is faithful, yet gentle. Ask God to help you remember what God wants for your life and to help you do those things well. Ask God to help you accept the challenges of a disciplined life and to give you joy in the process.

4

&

REFLECTION:
Looking Inward

Opening Prayer
>Slow me down, God. Still my body and my spirit, that
I may come to know myself and you more deeply. Amen.

Scripture Focus
>Return to me with all your heart. (Joel 2:12)

Daily Scripture Readings

Sunday	Psalm 1:2-3
Monday	Matthew 14:22-23
Tuesday	Psalm 19:14
Wednesday	Luke 10:38-42
Thursday	Isaiah 14:7
Friday	Psalm 46:10
Saturday	Luke 2:19

The Focus for Reflection

IT STARTED WITH PINBALL MACHINES—WONDROUS ARRAYS OF
color, light, and sound in which steel balls careened from one
obstacle to another. Then, in the early 1970s, the computer
video game revolution began. "Pong," the earliest video
game, was introduced. Two players controlled two electronic
paddles, bouncing a little electronic ball between them in a
simple game of Ping-Pong.

Looking back, this "revolutionary" new game was
basic—so basic that it is amusing. Yet, like a snowball rolling
down a hill, the concept of video games quickly gathered
momentum, and the next generations of computer games

developed quickly—each with more sophistication, speed, and complexity than the one before.

From pinball to "Pong" to "Pac-Man" to "Super Mario Brothers" and on to the next step in video—virtual reality—one simple constant remains: all of these games, no matter how sophisticated, are games of reaction. Whether you're playing with a steel ball in a pinball machine or responding to the electrical impulses of a complex computer program, you are reacting to something from the outside.

Being reactive is fine for video games. But careening from one situation to another, reacting to whatever presents itself in the outside world is no way to go through your daily life.

Instead, there is another way. It's called reflection—looking inward. Taking time for prayer and meditation is the way to move from being *re*active to being *pro*active. Instead of merely responding to circumstances, you give yourself a chance to reflect, to think things through, to pray for help and guidance.

That kind of "time out," or reflection, can help as you seek to share your faith, to plan for the future, to help a friend. It contributes to a spiritual and intellectual discipline that enables you to take more responsibility for your life and to achieve the goals to which you feel called.

When you feel life getting out of control, remember the lesson of the pinball. Instead of careening from one place to another, stop your activity. Sit quietly and reflect. Move from being reactive to being proactive.

Develop a faithful habit of daily reflection. Take some time to quiet your mind, to still your body, and to listen to your inner yearnings. Look inward often; you'll be surprised at the peace and direction that will come.

Points of Departure

♥ If you have a little quiet space in the morning, you can acknowledge your desire for love and reclaim your hope to remember love's presence during the hours to come. . . . The reflection can take many forms: journaling, writing poetry, drawing or painting, or just sitting prayerfully.
—From *The Awakened Heart* by Gerald G. May

♥ Decided at whatever cost of labour to start my diary rigorously again, wh. has been dropped during Schools, as I think the day to day continuity helps one to see the larger movement and pay less attention to each damned day in itself. . . .
—From *All My Road Before Me: The Diary of C. S. Lewis*

♥ My love and blessing for your Retreat. I hope and believe it will be a time of peace for you and, if you avoid all strain and let your soul slowly become tranquillized, you will begin, like the cats, to see a bit in the dark.
—From *The Letters of Evelyn Underhill*

♥ One who has been walking in a beautiful garden departs not willingly without gathering a few flowers to smell during the remainder of the day; thus ought we, when our soul has been entertaining itself by meditating on some mystery, to select one or two or three of those points . . . to think frequently on them, and smell them as it were spiritually during the course of the day.
—From *Introduction to the Devout Life* by Francis de Sales

Journaling: Ideas for Reflection
Which mode best describes the way you're living right now—reactive or proactive? Do you find yourself careening from one situation to another, or are you making time to sit quietly and reflect?

Think about ways you can build more reflective time into your life. What time of the day is best for you to be alone with your thoughts—first thing in the morning, noontime, mid-afternoon, sunset? Experiment with different times and places. Keep notes for yourself and see what you learn about your need for quiet reflection.

Prayers: For the World, for Others, for Myself
Ask God to still the busyness inside and around you. Take ten minutes to sit quietly and see what emerges. Pray that others—your family, friends, professors—may be gifted with reflective time.

5

&

STUDYING THE BIBLE

Opening Prayer
Guide and direct me as I study your Word. Amen.

Scripture Focus
One does not live by bread alone, but by every word that comes from the mouth of the Lord. (Deuteronomy 8:3)

Daily Scripture Readings

Sunday	Isaiah 55:10-11
Monday	John 8:31-32
Tuesday	Psalm 119:105
Wednesday	Matthew 4:1-4
Thursday	John 1:1-9
Friday	Ephesians 6:10-17
Saturday	James 1:22-25

The Focus for Reflection

IMAGINE USING THE BIBLE TO JUSTIFY TRAPPING HUMAN beings, stacking them in the cargo holds of ships, sailing them three thousand miles across a great ocean, stripping them naked, placing them on an auction block, and selling them into a lifetime of slavery. It happened, and not so very long ago.

People have used the Bible to justify bans on playing cards, going to movies, touring art museums, using make-up, wearing shorts. Their justification is that these things aren't in the Bible so people shouldn't be using them. (One wonders what they do with the non-biblical flush toilet!)

Some people use the Bible to deny others their civil rights; some to avoid the discipline of the medical and scientific models of discovery, understanding, and knowledge.

These are extreme examples of abusing the Bible, yet none of us is immune from this kind of misuse. It's really a matter of using care in our approach and interpretation.

First, your approach to the Bible must be one of discovery—learning about God through Jesus and the Hebrew scriptures, allowing growth to take place through God's grace, increasing your capacity to love. If it's not, then your "approach" is likely to be focused on manipulation, exploitation, and power politics.

Second, when you seek to interpret what you read in the Bible (and interpret you must), you have to decide what to take literally and what to take symbolically. This means you have to use your mind, the logical part of you, to understand what certain teachings mean.

Some cases in point: In Revelation, the great apocalyptic dragon knocks stars out of the sky with its tail (Rev. 12:4). Symbol, or a ten-million-mile-long dragon? What about Jesus' statement, "If your right eye offends you, pluck it out" (Matt. 5:29)? Is he speaking figuratively, or should we all go out and buy eye patches?

The Hebrew scripture calls for "an eye for an eye and a tooth for a tooth" (Exod. 21:24). Taken literally, what should you do if a blind guy with dentures hits you? As Tevye in *Fiddler on the Roof* observes, if that scripture is taken literally, the whole world would end up blind and toothless.

When Jesus says, "Whoever would be my disciple must take up the cross and follow me" (Matt. 16:24), was he calling for us literally to be crucified, or was he calling on us to be prepared to make sacrifices in our lives? It matters very much when you approach the Bible literally or when you approach it symbolically.

Finally, when you seek God through the Bible, you must be prepared to be changed. The Bible has an odd power to meet you where you are in your faith journey and to move you along—sometimes slowly, one step at a time, and sometimes with amazing speed. Approach the Bible with eagerness and openness, and God will meet you there. Seek to be changed by God's Word, and you will be guided along the way.

Points of Departure

♥ Bible study was not like examining history but like holding up a mirror to my own life, a mirror in which I sometimes saw things I was trying to keep hidden, even from myself.
—From *Returning: A Spiritual Journey* by Dan Wakefield

♥ Some people talk as if all you need to do to find God is to open the Bible and start reading. That certainly wasn't true for me. . . . A growing relationship with God had to come first, and then the Bible began to come alive.
—From *Finding God in the World* by Avery Brooke

♥ The Bible is a book of focus: God's graciousness, God's action with humanity, is focused in Jesus Christ.
—From *A Spirituality for the Long Haul* By Robert S. Bilheimer

♥ To sense the presence of God in the Bible, one must learn *to be present* to God in the Bible.
—From *God in Search of Man* by Abraham Joshua Heschel

♥ The authority of scripture becomes "real" in our lives as we open ourselves to hear the voice of the Master and seek to understand and do what God intends.
—From *Our Book: A United Methodist View of the Bible* by Horace Robert Weaver

Journaling: Ideas for Reflection

What is your relationship with the Bible like right now? Is it a book you pick up and read occasionally, or do you need to develop a more regular habit? Are there people in your faith community with whom you can study the Bible, people whose own faith journeys with the Bible can strengthen and support yours?

Think about the passages of scripture that are either most meaningful to you or most confusing. How can the use of your common sense inform a greater understanding of these passages?

Prayers: For the World, for Others, for Myself

Pray for guidance and direction as you study the Bible. Put yourself in God's hands and offer up to God your willingness to be challenged and changed by your study of the Bible. Keep in your prayers all those who struggle to understand and follow the Bible's teachings.

6

&

PRAYER:
Your Interior Life

Opening Prayer
Teach me to pray, O God. Make my prayers honest, open, and earnest. Amen.

Scripture Focus
In the morning, while it was still very dark, [Jesus] got up and went out to a deserted place, and there he prayed. (Mark 1:35)

Daily Scripture Readings
Sunday	Matthew 6:9-18
Monday	1 Kings 19:11-12
Tuesday	1 Samuel 1:12-18
Wednesday	Mark 14:32-42
Thursday	Romans 8:26-27
Friday	1 Thessalonians 5:17
Saturday	Philippians 4:6

The Focus for Reflection

HOWARD THURMAN CALLED PRAYER "THE HUNGER OF THE heart." For Reinhold Niebuhr, laughter was the beginning of prayer. Elizabeth Barrett Browning felt that our every wish was like a prayer to God.

Hunger, laughter, wishes—all these and more have been used to describe the experience of prayer. If you asked twenty different believers to describe prayer, you'd most likely get at least twenty different responses.

Why? Because the experience of prayer is as individual

and unique as each one of us is. Because prayer, as Australian cartoonist Michael Leunig says, is a "do-it-yourself ritual of connection, love, and transformation."

Meditation, contemplation, the breath prayer, centering prayer, prayers that use images instead of words— however it's done, prayer is simply our seeking a deeper relationship with God, and God's seeking a deeper relationship with us.

Whether your prayers are born of extreme crisis and despair or from the depths of joy and happiness, whether your prayers are eloquent or halting, whether you find yourself praying with complete faith or with great skepticism—it does not matter. What matters is the knowledge that God is always near, ready, waiting, listening.

So give yourself over to prayer. Keep at it, day in and day out. It does not matter *how* you pray; it only matters *that* you pray—because this practice of prayer will insure that, when it comes time for God to speak, *you* will be nearby— ready, waiting, listening.

Pray. Call out for forgiveness. Give thanks. Ask for guidance. Dream. Lay out your hopes and fears. Shout. Whisper. Talk. Listen. Laugh. Cry. Keep silence. Keep at it. It is all prayer. It is all your lifeline to God and God's lifeline to you.

Points of Departure

♥ Deep prayer opens the way for the fruits of the Spirit to grow in our life: love, joy, peace, kindness, benignity and chastity—attitudes and virtues that will greatly help us in our daily living out of our Christian life in the service of other and of our God.

—From *Centering Prayer* by M. Basil Pennington

♥ God answers sharp and sudden on some prayers,
And thrusts the thing we have prayed for in our face,
A gauntlet with a gift in't.
—From "Aurora Leigh" by Elizabeth Barrett Browning

♥ Prayer is not a substance to be isolated any more than people are; it is a process, an attitude of falling ever more deeply in love with life.
—From *On Becoming a Musical, Mystical Bear* by Matthew Fox

♥ I've always found time and a place for a "quiet time" to meditate, usually before I get ready for bed. To be at peace with God, and be ready for a new dawning.
—From an unpublished journal by Maude Fulcher Upchurch

♥ Above all things, Philothea, when you rise from meditation, remember the resolutions you have taken, and, as the occasion offers, carefully reduce them to practice that very day.
—From *The Introduction to the Devout Life* by Francis de Sales

♥ What counts is prayerfulness, not prayers.
—From *Gratefulness, the Heart of Prayer* by David Steindl-Rast

♥ The life of prayer, then, is a journey with God as well as toward God, a journey in which prayer becomes for those who pursue it as natural as breathing.
—From "Talking to God: An Intimate Look at the Way We Pray" by Kenneth L. Woodward, et. al.

Journaling: Ideas for Reflection

Take some time to reflect on your prayer life. Is praying easy or hard for you right now? Are you in the habit of daily conversation with God? What's the best time of day for you to schedule time for that conversation?

There are many forms of prayer. For some people, journal writing is a good form of prayer. For others, quieting the mind and body is important. Still others are able to pray while running or doing yoga. Make a list of the different ways in which you pray. Be mindful of those this week. Seek out new ways to be in touch with God through prayer.

Prayers: For the World, for Others, for Myself
    Ask for a deepened awareness of your communication
with God this week, and of God's communication with you.
Pray for mindfulness that your attitude be one of prayerfulness in all things. Ask God to be present with those around
you and in the wider world who struggle with their prayer
lives.

7
ఴ
Affirming Your Faith:
Your Witness Every Day

Opening Prayer

God, help me to match my actions with my beliefs so that who I am on the inside will be reflected on the outside. Amen.

Scripture Focus

You are the light of the world. (Matthew 5:14)

Daily Scripture Readings

Sunday	Joel 2:28-29
Monday	Revelation 3:15-16
Tuesday	Matthew 5:38-45
Wednesday	Proverbs 20:6-7
Thursday	1 John 3:1, 16-18
Friday	Matthew 28:19-20
Saturday	Hebrews 10:19-25

The Focus for Reflection

O GOD, YOU HAVE CALLED ME TO BE YOUR WITNESS IN THIS world each day. To answer that call, I need your constant presence and care. Strengthen my spirit that my confidence in you may encourage others.

I pray for consistency, clarity, and sincerity in my inward thoughts and outward actions, that I may become more pure in motive. If this in some way encourages others to seek the same, I will consider myself blessed by your grace.

Like Saint Francis, I want to be an instrument of your peace. I want to reflect love, faith, and hope in places where there is none. I want to find alternatives to the "eye for an eye" revenge mentality and learn to pray with enthusiasm for my enemies.

Help me to be the source of forgiveness you want me to be. I need your mercy, and that need reminds me to be merciful. Increase my ability to forgive others that they may catch a glimpse of your great love.

May my relationships with others be a way of reflecting your call to love my neighbor as I love myself. In this sometimes difficult work of fairness, I seek your strength and direction. Increase my hunger and thirst for your righteousness, that I may bear witness to your commitment to justice.

I pray that in my times of sadness, through my mourning, the comfort I receive from you may serve as a beacon of hope to others who mourn. May they know, through your kindness to me, the power you have to bring new life even out of despair.

When others insult me or try to embarrass me for my faith, help me to remember that my reward rests in you. Remind me that through faith and in time, I will come to see more clearly that which confuses me now.

O God, you call me to be your witness. You count on me to be a shining light, to bear witness like a city on a hill, to be for others a foundation for your love in this world. I often wonder why you chose me for this work, but in faith I will seek to serve you. Guide, direct, preserve, and protect me. Make me your faithful witness, every day. Amen.

Points of Departure

♥ As the truth of God has been made known by word, the love of God is made known by deeds.
—From *The Joy of Full Surrender* by Jean-Pierre de Caussade

♥ To look at our daily experience from the perspective of Scripture and Christian understandings puts our life in a new light and shows us what God is doing in our midst.
—From *Working Out Your Own Beliefs* by Douglas E. Wingeier

♥ "People's *deeds* I believe in, Miss—not their words."
—From *The Autobiography of Malcolm X*

♥ Lord, make me an instrument of thy peace;
   where there is hatred, let me sow love;
   where there is injury, pardon;
   where there is doubt, faith;
   where there is despair, hope;
   where there is darkness, light;
   and where there is sadness, joy.

O Divine Master,
   grant that I may not so much seek
to be consoled as to console;
to be understood, as to understand;
to be loved, as to love;
for it is in giving that we receive,
it is in pardoning that we are pardoned,
and it is in dying that we are born to eternal life.
—Saint Francis of Assisi

♥ A sacred deed is where earth and heaven meet.
—From *God in Search of Man* by Abraham Joshua Heschel

♥ Faith is not just the acceptance of abstract propositions about God; it is the total surrender of ourselves to God.
—From *The Heart of the World* by Thomas Keating

♥ It may sound strange to suggest that training one's mind to think is a form of witnessing, but thinking is an inner activity and is an important one when it comes to witnessing. Most of the television witnessing is mindless stuff and is a good example of the need for thinking Christian witnesses. Be one of them.
—From "Ten Ways to Share Your Faith on Campus" by Stewart A. Jackson and Anne Mitchell

---

Journaling: Ideas for Reflection
Think about people whose lives have had a positive influence on yours. As you consider each one, reflect on the qualities and values their lives embodied. How did their beliefs get lived out in their daily lives?

Look at the actions and attitudes that make up your daily witness. In what areas is your witness strong? Where is there inconsistency between what you believe and how you act? What can you do to gain more consistency and clarity in your daily witness?

Prayers: For the World, for Others, for Myself

As preparation for prayer this week, read the Beatitudes (Matt. 5:1-16). In your prayers, lift up places and situations in the world that need your witness and the witness of other believers. Pray that God will strengthen you and others in faith communities around the world to be good witnesses to love, hope, and justice. Ask for courage, commitment, and consistency in your witness.

8
ℰ
COPING WITH LONELINESS

Opening Prayer
  Sometimes, God, I feel lonely. In these times, watch over me, guide me, and comfort me with your presence. Amen.

Scripture Focus
  O God, do not be far from me. (Psalm 71:12)

Daily Scripture Readings
Sunday	Matthew 27:45-46
Monday	Psalm 22
Tuesday	Psalm 13
Wednesday	John 16:32
Thursday	Matthew 28:20
Friday	John 14:18
Saturday	Psalm 23

The Focus for Reflection

HAVE YOU EVER BEEN LONELY? NOT JUST ALONE, BUT downright lonely?
  It happens to all of us at one time or another. This occasional loneliness is a very normal experience. Sometimes life is such that loneliness is the only normal response to have. That kind of loneliness—short-term, occasional—is the kind you just wait out, knowing that it will end, knowing that the lonely feeling will go away.
  It's another kind of loneliness that is more troubling. The kind that often has you feeling lonely even when you are with a group of friends. The deep, pervasive loneliness that

causes you to push away the very people you care about. The loneliness that builds and builds, until you find yourself depressed and unwilling to make the effort to be with people.

When this kind of loneliness comes and stays, seek help. Talk with your minister or chaplain. Visit the student health center and talk with a counselor. Talk with a professor who feels approachable. Ask for help in finding a caring community of Christians.

Pray and ask God to help you find people who can guide you through this most difficult time. There are people out there who care, who are willing to help you.

When you come through to the other side of loneliness—and, with God's help, you will—remember how the healing came for you. Recall the things that were helpful for you, and keep a list of them for the next time loneliness comes—to you or to someone you know. It may be that you can be there to help when others find themselves caught in that same downward spiral of loneliness.

Asking for help when you are lonely is the first step toward helping yourself—and perhaps someone else— through loneliness, back to community. Share your feelings, and let God use others to bring you to wholeness again.

Points of Departure

♥ If in our loneliness we feel that God has abandoned us, we can say for ourselves what Jesus repeated to the Pharisees: "The One who sent me is with me. [God] has not left me alone." (John 8:29)
—From "The Man in the Santa Claus Suit" by Henry Fehren

♥ That night [my first Christmas Eve away from home], I learned the use of loneliness. That it sometimes is the push that sends us into the unknown where a fuller life is waiting.
—From "The Jumping Dove" by William Bryant Logan

♥ Lacking the inner resources to totally heal our loneliness, we turn to God, and that in itself is a spiritual benefit to loneliness.
—From "Where Can Loneliness Lead?" by Charlene Scott

♥ Giving [to others] is as effective as an anti-depressant. It is salve for wild attacks of loneliness, fear, and despair. It reconfirms that each of us *does* belong, that we are all interconnected.
—From *Random Acts of Kindness*

♥ As I turn my being toward the dark heavens, I practice the conversion of my loneliness to prayer. . . . I turn in longing toward God. . . .

Is it possible that beyond the enfolding darkness the Lord cries out to me with longing?
—From "Praying My Loneliness" by Suzanne Guthrie

Journaling: Ideas for Reflection

Think of a time when you were lonely. What did that loneliness feel like? Were you able to ask for help in getting through it? If so, where did the help come from?

What are some things that work for you when you feel lonely? Make a list of those things and keep it nearby.

Prayers: For the World, for Others, for Myself

Pray for persons who are lonely, asking that they and you be given the strength to reach out to someone and ask for help. If you are feeling alone right now, offer those feelings to God. In your prayer, imagine God's arms around you, holding you close and comforting you.

9

ॐ

INTERNAL AFFAIRS:
Caring for Your Body

Opening Prayer

I am grateful, Creator God, for the body you have given me. Amen.

Scripture Focus

My heart and my flesh sing for joy to the living God. (Psalm 84:2)

Daily Scripture Readings

Sunday	Genesis 1:31
Monday	Isaiah 40:28-31
Tuesday	Luke 4:1-11
Wednesday	1 Corinthians 6:15, 19-20
Thursday	1 Corinthians 12:14-26
Friday	Ephesians 4:15-16
Saturday	Philippians 4:8-9

The Focus for Reflection

YOU KNOW THE LITANY: EAT AT LEAST FIVE FRUITS AND vegetables a day. Drink plenty of water. Exercise three to five times a week. Avoid alcohol and other drugs. Get adequate rest. Keep a daily balance between work and play.

It's called caring for your body. But that is a little trickier than you might think.

When the New Testament refers to body, it often uses the Greek word *soma*. The notion of *soma* encompasses the whole person—body, mind, emotions, will. In this New

Testament way of understanding, it is impossible to separate body from soul. Each is inextricably bound up with the other.

Because your body and your spirit are so intertwined, caring for your body not only means eating right and exercising—it also means learning to listen to your body in a new way. It means learning to listen to the *wisdom* of your body, for your body will give you signals about what kind of care it needs.

Richard Strozzi Heckler in *The Anatomy of Change* makes the point that we may know a lot about the nourishment that comes from proper diet and still remain ignorant of the information about nourishment that comes from somewhere deep within us. We may, he says, know that we need to jog for exercise, but we can run miles every day and continue to be out of touch with what our body is trying to tell us it needs.

Caring for your body, then, means being *connected* with it, aware of feelings, sensations, and the messages it is constantly sending you. Caring for your body means living *through* your body, not just *in* it.

Many of us are in touch—truly connected—with our bodies only when we get sick, fatigued, or stressed. In truth, it's often because we have ignored our bodies in the first place that we end up sick or tired.

In caring for your body, pay attention not only to what you put into it, but also to what you expect out of it. Respect the wisdom of your body. The more in tune you are with how your body feels, the more you listen to your body, the more your body will be able to tell you what it needs.

You are wonderfully made. Care for your body. Respect its wisdom. Follow its leading.

Points of Departure

♥ As the body is clad in the cloth, and the flesh in the skin, and the bones in the flesh, and the heart in the whole, so are we, soul and body, clad in the Goodness of God, and enclosed.
—From *Revelations of Divine Love* by Juliana of Norwich

♥ The human body is an immense source of imagination, a field on which imagination plays wantonly. The body is the soul presented in its richest and most expressive form.
—From *Care of the Soul* by Thomas Moore

♥ Some say the soul informs the body. But what if we were to imagine for a moment that the body informs the soul. . . . Do we wish to spend a lifetime allowing others to detract from our bodies, judge them, find them wanting?
—From *Women Who Run with the Wolves* by Clarissa Pinkola Estés

♥ Advertising has spent billions of dollars trying to glamorize the "sip and puff" [alcohol and tobacco] lifestyle in America, but don't believe a word. It is far from glamorous.
—From *Temple Maintenance* by James P. Gills

♥ As I stepped up my own intake of alcohol and drugs during those years I of course blotted out the spiritual perceptions and impulses that were actually the very qualities and forces that might have begun to fill the emptiness and heal the pain.
—From *Returning: A Spiritual Journey* by Dan Wakefield

♥ You cannot nourish yourself if you hate the body you live in.
—From *The Woman's Comfort Book* by Jennifer Louden

Journaling: Ideas for Reflection

In *Prayer and Our Bodies,* Flora Slosson Wuellner notes that, while we pray for peace in the world and in our lives, we are often at war with our bodies. How do you feel about your own body? Are you able to accept yourself as you are now, or do you find yourself constantly criticizing your body? Are there parts of your body you need to make peace with?

Are you attentive to what your body needs— emotionally, physically, spiritually? How "in touch" with your body are you? In what ways do your daily habits of work, rest, nutrition, and exercise allow you to "glorify God" in your body? What areas have room for improvement?

Prayers: For the World, for Others, for Myself

This week, do what Wuellner suggests—pray for peace both in the world and between you and your body. Ask God to help you accept your body as it is and to motivate you to take better care of it. Spend some time in prayer listening for messages your body may be sending you about what you need to do for it.

10

&

TIME:
The Daily Challenge

Opening Prayer
Bless all the hours of my day, Eternal God. May I come to celebrate all time as your holy gift. Amen.

Scripture Focus
My times are in your hand. (Psalm 31:15)

Daily Scripture Readings

Sunday	Genesis 2:1-3
Monday	Ecclesiastes 3:1-8
Tuesday	1 Thessalonians 5:1-11
Wednesday	Exodus 20:8-11
Thursday	Mark 13:24-26, 32-33
Friday	2 Peter 3:8
Saturday	Psalm 9:1-2

The Focus for Reflection

HAVE YOU NOTICED THE DIFFERENCE IN YOUR MOOD, ATTITUDE, and personality in times when you're in a rush as opposed to times when you're in no hurry and feel no pressure from the clock?

At a university in the northeast, fifteen seminary students volunteered to be part of a study. They had no idea what it was about.

The fifteen were split into three groups. The first group received notes in an envelope telling them that they had ten minutes to get to a certain place across the campus. They were told not to waste time, but to leave immediately. It was very important, the instructions said, to get to the assigned place on time. This group was labeled the "high hurry" group.

The second group was given thirty minutes to reach the assigned place across campus. They were told thirty minutes was plenty of travel time, but they were warned not to linger too long on the way. This group was the "medium hurry" group.

The third group, the "low hurry" group, was given the entire afternoon to take the assigned route across campus.

None of the fifteen ministers-in-training knew that drama students were stationed at different points along the route. These drama students acted out different distress scenes as the seminarians crossed their paths. One was sobbing loudly, his head in his hands. One acted as though he was passed out, face down in the dirt. A third showed obvious signs of physical distress, nausea, and groaning.

The results of the study were stunning. They point in a powerful way to the moral nature of time management.

Of the "high hurry" group, not one person stopped to help any of the drama students in any way. Only two of the "medium hurry" group tried to give aid at some point in their travels. Of the "low hurry" group, every one of the five stopped at least once to offer assistance.

The implications of this study are profound:

• Those of us who are too tightly scheduled are in danger of "having no time" to help those in our path who need our help. We are unable to heed Christ's call to be neighbor to others.

• Those of us who have too many time commitments, too many things to do, eliminate our ability to handle the unexpected in our lives. We risk missing God's unexpected appearances before us.

• Those of us who fill our days, hours, and minutes too full rob ourselves of the time we need to develop strong relationships with others, with ourselves, and with God.

Time *is* a moral issue. Take time each day to treat your hours and minutes as gifts from God. Life is too precious to always be on the run.

Points of Departure

♥ Time is a spiritual concept.
—From *I'd Like to Call for Help, But I Don't Know the Number* by Abraham J. Twerski

♥ Spiritually aware people try to stay in touch with the present moment, trusting in the paradox that time will expand to encompass our needs, if only we wait for it.
—From "The Campus, the Spirit, and Health" by Malcom Burson, Jean Lappa, Cathy Taft, Frank Murray, and Thomas Chittick

♥ I have a fantasy of being more like the lilies of the valley, a fantasy of quietness. Sometimes, the fantasy is nothing more than a memory trace of a country road, along which I move, flurrying the tall weeds through my fingers, and thinking about nothing much—that in-between time, in which the soul refuels and regenerates. But we have so little time of that kind. We've become underdeveloped on the receptive side.
—From *Lost in Translation* by Eva Hoffman

♥ The Amish understand that it's not rushing through tasks to achieve a series of goals that is satisfying; it's experiencing each moment along the way.
—From *Plain and Simple* by Sue Bender

♥ To allow oneself to be carried away by a multitude of conflicting concerns, to surrender to too many demands, to commit oneself to too many projects, to want to help everyone in everything is to succumb to violence.
—From *Conjectures of a Guilty Bystander* by Thomas Merton

Journaling: Ideas for Reflection

Were you surprised by the results of the study cited in the essay? Have you noticed a difference in the way you relate to people when you're in a hurry?

If you had "more time," who would you spend it with? What would you do?

Who or what are you currently neglecting because you feel pressed for time? How could you free up more time to address those needs?

Prayers: For the World, for Others, for Myself
Make a conscious effort to allow more time for prayer
this week. Pray for an awareness of time as God's gift. Offer
your time to God, and ask for guidance in discerning how to
use your time each day.

11

&

MONEY:
Making Sense of It All

Opening Prayer

God, you call both rich and poor to worship you. Help me to understand how to use money in faithful ways. Amen.

Scripture Focus

A generous person will be enriched, and one who gives water will get water. (Proverbs 11:25)

Daily Scripture Readings

Sunday	Matthew 6:25-33
Monday	Deuteronomy 15:10-11
Tuesday	Proverbs 17:1
Wednesday	Proverbs 22:9
Thursday	Matthew 19:16-22
Friday	Mark 12:41-44
Saturday	Deuteronomy 8:11-18

The Focus for Reflection

IN ANCIENT EGYPT, PEOPLE WERE BURIED WITH THEIR PERSONAL possessions and financial wealth, under the assumption that these things would be helpful to them in the afterlife.

Tevye, the burdened father in the musical *Fiddler on the Roof* asked of God, "You made many, many poor people. I realize, of course, that it's no shame to be poor, but it's no great honor either. So what would have been so terrible if I had a small fortune?"

In the book of Matthew, Jesus tells his disciples that it would be "easier for a camel to go through the eye of a needle than for someone who is rich to enter the kingdom of God" (Matt. 19:24).

At the same time that we note pockets of incredible greed in this country, we also discover that no country in the world outdoes the United States for charitable donations.

Money, and our attitudes toward it, are very confusing. Wending your way through the possibilities and the pitfalls surrounding money can be precarious. Maybe the following observations will help.

First, the drive to acquire money can become addictive. For some people, earning all the money they can becomes their number one goal, and the costs are dear. As you set out to "earn a living," ask yourself this basic question: "What is my drive to acquire money costing me—in terms of relationships, career choice, physical and psychological health?" It's important to know the answer to that question all along the way so that you can make informed choices about your work life.

Second, the balance between income and outgo is an extremely important spiritual concern. If you overextend your financial resources, you will find that every day holds worry about how much money you have, how much you need, and how to reconcile the difference between the two. The spiritual discipline of reducing your material needs results in much greater freedom when it comes to earning and managing money.

Third, it matters what you do with your money. Giving away part of what you earn honors the biblical understanding that everything you have—including your ability to earn money—comes, in fact, from God. Your stewardship of money needs to include the spiritual discipline of sharing what you have with others—the church, the community, those in need nearby and around the world.

Finally, the amount of money you have can influence your relationship with God. In his public television special about the hymn "Amazing Grace," Bill Moyers interviews an old man who believes that having either too little or too much money makes it hard to experience God's grace—to appreciate the gospel's message of God's nurturing love for us and of our need for God's forgiveness. As you deal with money—whether out of extreme poverty, excessive riches, or somewhere in between—pay attention to its impact on your experience of God's grace.

Points of Departure

♥ The point I had wanted to make was that money can buy almost anything we want—the problem being that we tend to want only the things that money can buy.
—From *Money and the Meaning of Life* by Jacob Needleman

♥ Recuérdate, no todo lo que brilla es oro. [Remember, not all that shines is gold.]
—Mexican proverb

♥ Perhaps Money, in America, is a force so extreme as to become a religious force, a confusing deity, which demands either idolatry or a spiritual education.
—From *Lost in Translation* by Eva Hoffman

♥ The apostle Paul's exhortation to "be content" (1 Timothy 5:6-8) has great relevance to the modern pressure to "buy now pay later."
—From *Debt* by Roy McCloughry and Andrew Hartropp

♥ Enjoyment is not measured by what flows in, but by what flows over. The smaller we make the vessel of our need for use, the sooner we get the overflow we need for delight.
—From *Gratefulness, the Heart of Prayer* by David Steindl-Rast

♥ Your goal is to achieve *financial reality*—a state of awareness where you know how much money you have, you know how much money you owe, and you know not to owe more than you have.
—From "Money Management 101: An Introduction to Financial Reality" By Nedra Lambert

---

Journaling: Ideas for Reflection
Identify times in your life when you felt in control of your finances. Were there times when you felt your finances controlled you? Reflect on these feelings. What effect did each of these situations have on your relationship with God?

Do you know someone who seems to be controlled by money or by a strong desire for it? What is it like to be around this person?

The less money you need, the more freedom you have. In what ways can you cut back on your need for money? How would those cutbacks increase your freedom to choose what you do with your time and what you might do for a career?

Prayers: For the World, for Others, for Myself
Pray for a balanced attitude toward money. Try seeing what you have as enough. Remember in your prayers those who are so rich they feel no need for God, and those who are so poor that they lack the basic necessities of life. Ask God to guide you in the right use of your money.

12
&

GRADES:
Grace and Judgment

Opening Prayer
Grant me grace and peace as I seek to learn. Amen.

Scripture Focus
Therefore the Lord waits to be gracious to you. (Isaiah 30:18)

Daily Scripture Readings

Sunday	Mark 9:33-35
Monday	Galatians 5:22-26
Tuesday	Romans 12:3-8
Wednesday	Proverbs 24:13-14
Thursday	1 Corinthians 12:4-11
Friday	1 Peter 2:9-10
Saturday	Romans 14:13

The Focus for Reflection

HAVE YOU EVER HAD A TEACHER OR PROFESSOR WHO TAUGHT you as much about life outside the classroom as they taught you about their subject area inside the classroom? I was fortunate enough to have two such professors in my life— Ellen Hoffman and Carlyle Marney. Both are now dead. They never met. But they would have liked each other, because they shared some basic convictions about education.

Hoffman was my undergraduate government professor. She loved things political. For many years, she worked on staff for a U.S. senator. She reveled in the study of government. She had an infectious laugh, a welcoming spirit, and a keen mind.

Marney was one of my preaching professors in graduate school. He was a crusty, down-to-earth Southern Baptist minister who liked to say, "Those who ordained me would take it back if they could." After a significant pause for effect, he'd add with glee, "But they can't."

He loved being able to integrate different academic disciplines. It thrilled him to help others see their interconnectedness. Most of all, he loved caring for and teaching other pastors.

Each of these professors gave me important insights into the world of grades and learning.

Hoffman, who had adopted two baby girls, once told me, "In the twenty-five years since I finished graduate school, no one has ever asked me what my grade point average was. And I've decided that as long as my daughters give a good effort at learning, their grades will take care of themselves. I want them to enjoy their years in college, not to be in constant turmoil trying to do everything perfectly."

Marney told all of his final semester theology students this about the degree we were about to earn: "Your degree won't be worth a plug nickel in five years if you don't use what you have learned here. No matter what your grades are, if you haven't learned how to ask questions and search for the answers, your degree will be worthless. Knowing how to ask questions, knowing how to study, being willing and able to search for the resources to answer your questions—these are the keys to judging your degree."

You see, Ellen Hoffman and Carlyle Marney understood that learning was much more than exam scores and grade point averages. They understood that God speaks a great word of grace to all who would hear it. Their advice: "Give college a good effort. Let the grades take care of themselves. Have fun. Learn now how to find the resources you will need after you graduate. Let go of your anxiety about grades, and discover the joy of learning. It's all part of loving God with your mind."

That's good counsel for college and a good perspective for all your life's journey.

Points of Departure

♥ Not knowing, and learning to be comfortable with not knowing, is a great discovery.
—From *Plain and Simple* by Sue Bender

♥ As wise women and men in every culture tell us: The art of life is not controlling what happens to us, but *using* what happens to us.
—From *Revolution from Within: A Book of Self-Esteem* by Gloria Steinem

♥ Motivation may indeed come from wells of strength and purpose within; but it also comes from confronting the realities of scholastic probation, creditors, divorce, and defeat.
—From "In Praise of Hard Knocks" by Wendy Reid Crisp

♥ Perhaps the most important thing I learned is that the artist is not separate from the work and therefore cannot judge it.
—From *Two-Part Invention: The Story of a Marriage* by Madeleine L'Engle

♥ The deeper we search the nearer we arrive at knowing that we do not know.
—From *God in Search of Man* by Abraham Joshua Heschel

♥ After all, what is education but a process by which a person begins to learn how to learn?
—From *Dear Me* by Peter Ustinov

Journaling: Ideas for Reflection

What's your current comfort/anxiety level about grades? Are you able to approach your studies motivated to learn, or are you caught up in worry about your grade point average? How can you find a good balance between the focus on learning and the focus on grades?

Prayers: For the World, for Others, for Myself
   Pray for those involved in the enterprise of education—classmates, professors, administrators. Ask that you, and all these others, be guided by a love of learning. Pray for perspective when it comes to the judgment of grades.

13

ಬಿ
STRENGTHENING YOUR FAITH:
A Lover's Quarrel

Opening Prayer
God, I bring all my questions and doubts to you. Hear me in my struggle to understand. Amen.

Scripture Focus
Consider and answer me, O Lord my God! (Psalm 13:3*a*)

Daily Scripture Reading
Sunday	Genesis 32:22-31
Monday	Judges 6:11-18
Tuesday	Job 7:11
Wednesday	John 20:24-29
Thursday	1 Corinthians 13:12
Friday	2 Corinthians 4:7-11
Saturday	John 3:1-9

The Focus for Reflection

MANY PEOPLE BELIEVE THAT THE OPPOSITE OF LOVE IS HATE, but that's not true. The opposite of love is apathy—not caring.

Robert Frost, the legendary poet, understood that. He had these words engraved on his tombstone: "I had a lover's quarrel with the world." Frost understood that the intensity of his love for the world guaranteed that he would sometimes quarrel with it. That quarrel, for him, was evidence of his love.

A similar dynamic exists in your relationship to the faith. If you can get angry with God, agitated at the church, cynical about the faith, questioning of Christianity's tradition, then you are also a spiritual lover. Doubts and questions and quarrels are signs of a healthy faith. You're not in trouble when you doubt—you're only in trouble when you stop caring.

Perhaps you know someone who always seems eager to tangle over the faith, the church, things spiritual—someone who is ready to ask the cynical question or to challenge traditional beliefs.

Don't be put off or fooled by them. No matter how hard these "quarrelers" may try to put distance between themselves and the faith community, their emotional involvement betrays them. They are in reality spiritual lovers, caring so much about their relationship with God that they dare to argue with God.

Be patient with people like this. God uses time and reflection to heal these lover's quarrels, and a stronger faith emerges because of them.

If the one having the lover's quarrel with God is you, be patient with yourself. God does find ways for the quarrels to become foundations for a stronger faith.

Let your questions, doubts, and frustrations come. What they reveal about you is the lover, the fighter, who will not let go. God can handle your honest feelings and your quarrels. God can take your hurts and disappointments and use them to strengthen your faith.

Points of Departure

♥ Doubt is simply an experience of our limits, the limits of our wisdom amid the complexity of life.
—From *Choices: Making Right Decisions in a Complex World* by Lewis B. Smedes

♥ There is no faith at first sight. A faith that comes into being like a butterfly is ephemeral. [One] who is swift to believe is swift to forget.
—From *God in Search of Man* by Abraham Joshua Heschel

♥ It takes both believers and skeptics to make a civilization.
—From *The Vital Balance* by Karl Menninger

♥ "You know," said Ellen Cherry, "I can't figure out the popularity of those cults. Okay, so people can get somebody else to do their thinking for them, what is the big appeal?"
—From *Skinny Legs and All* by Tom Robbins

♥ A college education isn't worth very much if all you get out of it is a reinforcing of what you already know and believe.
—From *College: Getting in and Staying in* by D. Bruce Lockerbie and Donald R. Fonseca

♥ To say "I am angry with God" is to make a bold affirmation of faith. It is to say "I believe in God, and I am willing to share my strongest feelings with God."
—Thomas C. Ettinger

Journaling: Ideas for Reflection

Have you ever felt anger, frustration, or doubts about your faith? When you do, who do you talk with about them? What would it feel like to go directly to God with your anger and doubts?

The psalm writers were not afraid to express their deepest thoughts and feelings to God. Try writing your own psalm, bringing to God any doubts or frustrations you may be feeling about your relationship with God right now.

In the quote above, Karl Menninger said that it takes both skeptics and believers to make a civilization. At different times, each of us is either a skeptic or a believer. Which most accurately describes you right now, and why?

Prayers: For the World, for Others, for Myself
In your prayers this week, risk sharing your deepest thoughts and feelings with God—both the positive ones and the negative ones. Explore what happens when you do this.

14

&

GRACE:
The Amazing Gift

Opening Prayer
Keep me mindful of your grace this week, loving God.
Help me to be an instrument of your grace for others. Amen.

Scripture Focus
For all of you share in God's grace. . . . (Philippians
1:7)

Daily Scripture Readings
Sunday	John 1:14-18
Monday	Luke 15:11-24
Tuesday	2 Corinthians 5:16-21
Wednesday	Romans 5:18-21
Thursday	Hebrews 4:14-16
Friday	Ephesians 2:4-9
Saturday	1 Timothy 1:12-17

The Focus for Reflection

I'LL NEVER FORGET THE OLD GREEN FORD STATION WAGON MY
family had when I was growing up. Made in the 1950s, it was
one of those "gas guzzlers" that families bought back then to
cart around all the kids and their assorted pets.

My best memories of that station wagon are of the
times we went to the drive-in movies together—me, Mom and
Dad, and my sisters. Mom and Dad in the front seat, us kids
in the back, the scratchy metal speaker hung in the window,
the movie on a giant screen in front of us, and that old station
wagon filled with blankets and pillows for us to sleep on.

I don't recall any of the movies we saw during those early years; I fell asleep halfway through most of them. But what I do remember—what will never leave me—is the special feeling I had when, at the end of the evening after he'd driven us home, my father would pick me up and carry me gently into the house to my bedroom. He would quietly lay me in my bed and tuck me in for the night. I got such a warm, safe, and loved feeling.

I'm in my forties now, and sometimes I still wish it were possible for my father to take me in his arms, carry me safely to bed, and tuck me in. I know that he can't, but I still wish. . . .

When I think of God's love for me, the first thing that comes to mind are those feelings from my childhood about that old car, those drive-in movies, and my father's gentle care.

When I think of John 14:3, the passage in which Jesus says he is going to prepare a place for us with God, I believe I know what to expect—in the very depths of my spirit, the memory of my father's care for me shows, in some small way, the care God has for us.

The feeling of being supported, carried, held in warmth, and loved. That, for me, is grace.

Points of Departure

♥ I know love is a gift because I have experienced more love in my life than I could ever have deserved or earned. I cannot take credit for any of it. It is all grace.
—From *The Awakened Heart* by Gerald G. May

♥ This was shewed: that in falling and in rising we are ever preciously kept in one Love.
—From *Revelations of Divine Love* by Juliana of Norwich

♥ Grace expresses the character of God. God had the freedom to remain unrelated; instead God was moved to create a universe, to situate humans in it, and to move toward them.
—From "Grace" by Martin Marty in *A New Handbook of Christian Theology*

♥ To pray without ceasing, on every possible occasion, means that we are to be in a state of remembrance of what God has done and is doing for us.
—From *The Breath of Life* by Ron DelBene with Mary and Herb Montgomery

♥ Let thy hearts be at peace in this serene and healing place, for here the Lord Christ will refresh you, here he will lift the heavy burden from your minds and in thy hearts he will breathe renewed joy and quietude.
—From *Letters of the Scattered Brotherhood* edited by Mary Strong

---

Journaling: Ideas for Reflection

As you look back, what signs of God's grace in your own life can you identify? How have teachers, friends, ministers or parents been instruments of grace for you? When have you felt grace as the experience of being "supported, carried, held in warmth, and loved"?

How is the story of the Prodigal Son (Luke 15:11-24) a story about God's grace? How is that story the story of God's relationship with you?

How might God be calling you to be an instrument of grace in other people's lives?

Prayers: For the World, for Others, for Myself

In your prayer time, sit quietly and recall God's gifts of grace to you. Lift up before God concerns in your life and in the life of the world that need God's touch of grace. Look through one day's newspaper to identify people in the world you want to remember in prayer. Pray to be guided this week that you may be a channel for God's grace to others.

15

ಐ
LOVING YOURSELF AS
GOD LOVES YOU

Opening Prayer
Help me to understand and accept the love you have for me, gracious God. Amen.

Scripture Focus
You are precious in my sight, and honored, and I love you. (Isaiah 43:4)

Daily Scripture Readings
Sunday	Luke 10:25-28
Monday	John 8:1-11
Tuesday	Psalm 139:1-12
Wednesday	John 10:11-18
Thursday	Matthew 18:12
Friday	John 3:16
Saturday	1 Peter 5:7

The Focus for Reflection

ALMOST EVERYONE HAS A FAVORITE PART OF THE DAY. Perhaps yours is the morning, with a brilliant sun rising in the sky, a brisk jog or walk at breakfast time, the beginning of a new day. Maybe it's the nighttime that beckons you. A late bedtime, hanging out, vegging on TV movies, putting in some study time. Or it could be your exercise time, when your body feels that rush of endorphins and you feel alive and renewed.

For me, it's sunset. Dusk. When the day is done and all nature transitions from light to dark. This is, for me, the most relaxing time of day. Whenever I can, I like to be outside for at least part of that two-hour changeover. I feel I'm somehow part of it all: the setting sun, gentle breezes, first star and planet, the ever-changing moon, and the slowly-falling darkness.

My body, mind, and spirit hear the echo of God's creation passed down through millions of years. "Day is done. You are loved. Seek the peace and rest I want you to have."

The more I allow myself to transition with the evening, the better I am able to review my day and plan for tomorrow. Then I can simply make peace with who I am, let go, and trust myself to be supported and used by God.

One of the best ways for you to bless the Lord is to take some time for yourself in your favorite part of the day. Receive from God all the re-creation you can, and dedicate your energies to giving thanks, letting this time touch you deeply. God loves you. God has given you the gifts of relaxation and refreshment. Begin to love yourself as God loves you by accepting those gifts.

You are a wondrous child of God. Love yourself as God loves you by discovering, nurturing, and celebrating your favorite time of day. Let it become more and more a part of your spiritual life. Accept yourself. Accept God's gifts. Rejoice. Give thanks. Be at peace.

Points of Departure

♥ Good spiritual health helps us see ourselves through God's eyes as unique and special persons.
—From "The Campus, the Spirit, and Health" by Malcom Burson, Jean Lappa, Cathy Taft, Frank Murray, Thomas Chittick

♥ How do you really feel about yourself? Are you at least as kind to yourself as you are to your friends?
—From *An Ascent to Joy: Transforming Deadness of Spirit* by Carol Ochs

♥ My dear friend Alex Haley has a saying, which I am putting into practice today—"Find the good and praise it."
—From "Find the Good and Praise It" by Lamar Alexander

♥ We still have the need to know that we are lovable and capable of loving. . . . We need to be able to be assured that, when people go away, they'll come back. We need to know that we don't have to be perfect in order to be of value.
—Fred Rogers in "This 'Neighborhood' Still Feels Like Home," an interview by Tom Ensign

♥ None of us is perfect. . . . One of the most compassionate things we can do for ourselves is not take those imperfections too seriously.
—From *The Healing Power of Humor* by Allen Klein

Journaling: Ideas for Reflection

What is your favorite part of the day? How often do you take the time to savor it?

Make a list of activities, places, and people that enable you to feel God's peace and acceptance. How often do you make time to do these things, visit these places, and see these people?

As you keep your journal, make note of how you are affected on the days you take time for yourself. Are you more at peace, more centered, more able to accept yourself? What happens on the days you don't take this time?

Prayers: For the World, for Others, for Myself
Give to God in prayer those parts of yourself that you need to accept in order to be at peace. Imagine God's loving presence around you, and rest in that love.

16

&

COPING WITH FAILURE

Opening Prayer

Be with me through my successes and my failures, that I may grow in your wisdom and strength. Amen.

Scripture Focus

The steadfast love of the Lord never ceases. (Lamentations 3:22)

Daily Scripture Readings

Sunday	Psalm 143:7-10
Monday	Luke 22:31-34
Tuesday	Colossians 3:1-4
Wednesday	Ezekiel 37:1-14
Thursday	Deuteronomy 31:7-8
Friday	1 Corinthians 1:26-27
Saturday	Ephesians 4:32

The Focus for Reflection

FAILURE. IT COMES FROM THE LATIN WORD FALLERE AND IT originally meant to disappoint.

Each of us knows what that disappointment is like—to give something a good effort and to have that effort met not with success, but with failure.

The disappointment that comes with failure is bitter, and many times you may be tempted to give up. But before you do, consider this: Dr. Seuss's book *And to Think That I Saw It on Mulberry Street* was rejected by twenty-three publishers before it was printed. *M*A*S*H*, by Richard Hooker, was rejected twenty-one times. Richard Bach's *Jonathan Livingston Seagull* was published by the nineteenth publisher he approached. In addition to their perseverance in the face of failure, all three of these authors have something else in common: Each of their books is among the top best-sellers in this century.

The Bible cites many examples of people who faced failure but refused to give up.

For many, many years, Sarah had been unable to conceive the child she and Abraham had been promised. In her old age, she gave birth to Isaac. Through him, Abraham and Sarah became the father and mother of a great people (Gen. 18:1-15; 21:1-8).

Peter, one of Jesus' disciples, faltered in his faith many times over the course of his life—most notably on the night before the crucifixion, when he denied three times that he even *knew* Jesus (Luke 22:54-62). Yet, Peter became the rock on which the church was built (Matt. 16:18).

Even Jesus experienced failure. Many times, the people who came to hear him misunderstood his message. When he preached in Nazareth, his hometown, people ran him out of town and tried to throw him off a cliff (Luke 4:16-30). Yet he, too, kept at it.

When you find yourself facing failure, take heart. As Samuel Johnson says, don't be ashamed of your failures. Instead, learn from them. Keep trying. Let your failures lead you to new paths.

And remember, even though failure is an inevitable part of being human, it is never the ultimate claim in your life. God's grace is the ultimate claim. It is God's grace that helps to pick you up when you fail. That same grace will carry you through whatever failures—of faith, of body, of mind—you come up against in the years ahead.

Points of Departure

♥ Failure is implicit in challenge. It wouldn't be a challenge if we knew we could do it.
—From *The Woman's Comfort Book* by Jennifer Louden

♥ If at first you don't succeed, you're about average.
—Ann Landers

♥ Thus it is a matter of facing up to our problems rather than avoiding them, of tackling them together and seeking together their solution.
—From *To Understand Each Other* by Paul Tournier

♥ It is in our own weakness and limitation that God comes to us, not in our strength, security, and certitude.
—From *A Blessed Weakness* by Michael Downey

♥ It's regrets that make painful memories.
—From *The Eden Express* by Mark Vonnegut

♥ The fear of failure and the illusion that we have to succeed in order to earn love can be a lifelong tyranny. Sometimes it is possible to see in retrospect that a failure which grieved you at the time was a necessary stage on the way to something else.
—From *Gateway to Hope: An Exploration of Failure* by Maria Boulding

Journaling: Ideas for Reflection

What do you think about Michael Downey's statement above that God comes to us in our own weakness and limitation? Take time to write about how that statement speaks to your life. Have you experienced God's presence in times when you came up against your limitations and felt like a failure? If so, what did that feel like? Did it help you to get up and start again? Why or why not?

Ask someone you admire and trust to talk with you about his or her own failures. Find out how that person handles the disappointment of failure. Many people say they have learned more from their failures than from their successes. How about for you? Can you recall times when you failed to achieve something you wanted to? Were these times learning experiences? If so, what did you learn?

Sometimes we set ourselves up for failure by having unreasonable expectations of ourselves. Reflect on your own expectations for yourself. Are there areas of your life in which your expectations need to be adjusted in order to become more reasonable? If so, what are those areas and what adjustments do you need to make?

Prayers: For the World, for Others, for Myself

Pray for people you know who are struggling with limitations. Do you know fellow students who are having a hard time in their classes? Are there members of your family who have experienced the setback of failure recently? Put these people on your prayer list, and pray that they be given the support and grace they need to persevere.

If you are facing a difficult situation, use your prayer time to remind yourself that God's love is there for you, whether you succeed or fail.

17
&

CHANGING MAJORS, CHOOSING A CAREER:
Listening for a Calling

Opening Prayer

Give me a discerning mind and an inventive spirit as I listen for your call, O God. Amen.

Scripture Focus

Whatever your hand finds to do, do with your might. (Ecclesiastes 9:10*a*)

Daily Scripture Readings

Sunday	Ephesians 4:11-13
Monday	Amos 7:14-15
Tuesday	Isaiah 6:1-8
Wednesday	Matthew 9:35-38
Thursday	Exodus 35:24-29
Friday	1 Corinthians 12:4
Saturday	1 Samuel 3:1-10

The Focus for Reflection

"WHAT'S YOUR MAJOR?" THAT'S THE COLLEGE VERSION OF "What do you want to be when you grow up?" If you've been asked the question once, you've probably been asked it a hundred times. How you answer it depends entirely on the circumstances in which you find yourself at any one particular time.

Some students I had classes with had decided early on exactly what their field of study would be, and they never veered from that initial course. There were others who majored in "undecided" as long as possible, chose a major only when they were forced to by school policy, and then changed majors two or three times before they graduated.

Some people know the career they want to pursue from the time they're ten years old. Others go through the traditional childhood litany of vocations—firefighter, doctor, astronaut, actor—and end up in college still unsure of what they want to do with their work lives.

Whichever category you fit, here are some things to think about:

• *Vocation* is from a Latin word that means "calling," and that's exactly what vocations are—callings to use your gifts and talents in the world. Prayerfully consider where the call of God is guiding and directing you. Joseph Campbell called it "following your bliss."

• Your choice of vocation has a powerful effect on your life—not just financially, but psychologically, emotionally, and spiritually. Yet, your life is much more than just your work. Seek balance between your work life and your life away from work.

• Gathering information about career opportunities, that is, "doing your homework," is essential. It can be hard work, but stick with it.

• The generation that came before you was told they could become anything they wanted to be if they worked at it. That's often not the case anymore. Because of the economy and the different job markets, you can no longer assume that if you choose a major, study hard, and complete your degree, a job will be waiting for you when you graduate. That's a tough realization to come to. Yet, not being able to manage your vocational choice the way students in decades past could does in some ways allow you to listen more closely for God's call in your life.

• Change of job or career is not failure. (Statistics show that many people change either their jobs or their careers more than once in their lifetimes.) In fact, changing careers often turns out to be a process of "fine tuning," of coming closer and closer to where you need to be. Disappointment, even failure, is sometimes the path toward finding the vocation that fits you best.

• Very little drains the spirit more than being in a vocation you do not like or you don't feel called to. Pay attention to how you feel about what you're studying in your major courses. That will give you clues about the work you need to be moving toward.

• We believe that everyone has a vocational calling. For some, that calling may be to work professionally in the church. For others, that calling may be to work in the secular world. Either way, your vocation is a sacred calling. If after reflection, study, counsel, and prayer, you feel led toward a certain vocation, give it your best effort. If sometimes a window of opportunity seems to close, stay the course. Perhaps a doorway of opportunity will open in its place.

"What's your major?" "What do you want to be when you grow up?" Even though we're both in our forties, we still sometimes wonder about those questions. As we wrestle with our callings, we remind ourselves that God's grace sustains us amidst our questions. As you wrestle with your calling, remind yourself of that, too.

Points of Departure

♥ God's will is not an impersonal blue-print for living forced on us by a capricious God and contrary to almost every inclination in us. God's will is our freedom. [God] wants us to discover what we really want and who we really are.
—From *God of Surprises* by Gerard W. Hughes

♥ Work is an important part of life, but it is not the whole of life. Moreover, the proper place of work in a person's life is an issue that must be posed anew from time to time, and may demand creative answers. Life is dynamic. It changes over time.
—From *The Fabric of This World* by Lee Hardy

♥ If we had perfect self-discernment before we began professional training, and we got trained in our hearts' desires, all would be well. But we lack such prescience. It often takes years for our hearts to speak.
—From *The Active Life* by Parker J. Palmer

♥ "If you're really good at something, I mean if there's nobody, or hardly anybody, who's as good as you are, then you've got to be serious about that. Don't mess around, for God's sake."
—From *A Separate Peace* by John Knowles

♥ Glorious labor! It both warms and nourishes those that are engaged in it.
—Jewish proverb

♥ In Benedictine spirituality, work is what we do to continue what God wanted done. . . . We work because the world is unfinished and it is ours to develop.
—From *Wisdom Distilled from the Daily* by Joan D. Chittister

♥ For vocation is an illusive and elusive thing. Maybe the only way to ever have it is to quit looking for it.
—From "Vocation as Grace" by Will D. Campbell in *Callings*

Journaling: Ideas for Reflection

Is there a vocational leaning you've had since you were a child? If so, what area is it in?

If you could choose without restraint what career to pursue, what would it be? Why?

Which category best describes where you are right now in choosing a major and a career—are you fairly sure of what you want to do, or are you still exploring lots of options? What people (friends, professors, your advisor, your campus minister, family) do you know who can help you in your search to find out what you want to do with your education? Name them.

If you think you've identified a vocation for yourself, what factors, besides finances, contributed to your choice?

Prayers: For the World, for Others, for Myself

Wherever you find yourself in relation to choosing a major and a career, use your prayer time to listen for God's calling in your life. Pray for guidance and direction. Ask God's blessing on all those who work, that their efforts may further the work God has begun in the world.

18

&

FRIENDSHIP

Opening Prayer

Steadfast God, help me to be steadfast and trustworthy in my friendships with others. Amen.

Scripture Focus

When I remember you in my prayers, I always thank my God. (Philemon 1:4)

Daily Scripture Readings

Sunday	Ruth 1:15-18
Monday	1 Samuel 18:1-4
Tuesday	John 15:12-15
Wednesday	Philippians 2:1-8
Thursday	Job 2:11-13
Friday	Proverbs 17:9,17
Saturday	Luke 22:28

The Focus for Reflection

MANY PEOPLE WILL CROSS YOUR PATH IN THE YEARS AHEAD. They will influence you, and you, in turn, will have an influence on their lives. Some of these people will become your friends. Some of these friendships will last a lifetime.

Such friendships are important, but be very clear about one thing: Every friendship you start will go through many changes, some of them quite radical. Some friendships may even end. Yet within each of us is the need, the inner will to seek, nurture, and value friendship, no matter what the risk. Given the benefits, friendship is clearly worth the risk.

It takes commitment, trust, nurture, and adjustment

for friendships to grow strong. Commitment—to be with someone for the long haul, through good times and bad. Trust—the two-way street of both trusting another and being trustworthy yourself. Nurture—the dedication of time and energy toward building the friendship. Adjustment—the willingness to be flexible and open, accepting changes in your friendship, and growing through those changes.

Most important of all, friendship demands forgiveness. There will be times of misunderstanding and hurt, especially in friendships that are very close. Be ready to forgive. Be ready to ask for forgiveness for yourself. Be sensitive to the healing power forgiveness can bring to friendship, and be gracious with it.

Sad, but true, not all people are trustworthy. You will no doubt find yourself involved with some of those people, and you will be hurt when these "friendships" end. Even trustworthy lifelong friendships carry their share of disappointments. But the rich blessing of friendship gives life a depth of meaning unlike anything else. Ask God to guide you, be willing to spend time developing friendships, and the treasured shelter of a good friend will be yours.

Points of Departure

♥ A bond grew between us. It grew quite strong because it grew from the depths, from the heart.
—From *A Blessed Weakness* by Michael Downey

♥ We have the saints to show us that these things are actually possible: that one human soul can rescue and transfigure another and can endure for it redemptive hardship and pain.
—From *Concerning the Inner Life* by Evelyn Underhill

♥ I knew that part of friendship consisted in accepting a friend's shortcomings, which sometimes included his [or her] parents.
—From *A Separate Peace* by John Knowles

♥ For without friends no one would choose to live, though [they] had all other goods.
—Aristotle

♥ Faithful friends are a sturdy shelter:
 Whoever finds one has found a treasure.
 —Sirach 6:14 (NRSV)

♥ I have discovered that different seasons in my life require different kinds of friendship and different levels of companionship.
—From *Seasons of Friendship* by Marjory Zoet Bankson

♥ Friends become for us a mirror on the self; and what we see there, whether it pleasures or pains us, helps to affirm those parts of self we like and respect and to change those whose reflection brings us discomfort.
—From *Just Friends* by Lillian B. Rubin

♥ One kind word can warm up three winter months.
—Japanese proverb

Journaling: Ideas for Reflection

What qualities do you bring to a friendship? What qualities do you look for in a friend? Compare the two lists.

Risk-taking is a part of all friendships. Under what circumstances would you take the risk of confronting a friend about some behavior, habit, or pattern you considered self-destructive or not in his or her best interest? Under what circumstances would you want a friend to confront you?

Prayers: For the World, for Others, for Myself

Pray for your friends—the ones you see every day, those from whom you are separated by distance, those with whom you've lost touch. Give thanks for the support and care of friends. Ask God's help in being a trustworthy friend. Lift up in prayer those who seek the support and care of good friends.

19

৵

LIFELONG RELATIONSHIPS

Opening Prayer
Give me courage and discernment, that I may love wisely and honestly. Amen.

Scripture Focus
To see your face is like seeing the face of God. (Genesis 33:10)

Daily Scripture Readings

Sunday	1 Corinthians 13
Monday	Ephesians 5:25-33
Tuesday	Song of Solomon 8:6-7
Wednesday	Genesis 29:18-20
Thursday	Mark 10:6-9
Friday	2 John 4-6
Saturday	Matthew 5:21-24

The Focus for Reflection

APPROXIMATELY ONCE EVERY FIVE YEARS, ON AVERAGE, Americans change their address. The reasons for these moves vary—going to school, changing jobs, getting married or divorced, changes in health or financial status—but the resulting disruption means one thing: Our ability to develop and maintain lifelong relationships is deeply affected.

With this kind of mobility, most of us will be lucky to have four or five relationships that will last a lifetime. Count them any way you want—friend, spouse, relative—you probably will be able to number them on one hand. Given these statistics, developing and nurturing long-term relationships becomes a priority.

But what is it that cements a relationship? What is it that enables people to stick with each other over the long haul? What is it that finally makes or breaks a relationship?

The key ingredient, it seems, is intimacy. That sounds simple enough until you start trying to define what it means. Is it physical, financial, material? Does it come from shared interests, beliefs, values? Can it be found in common hobbies, common likes, common dislikes?

Not really. True intimacy—intimacy that will sustain a relationship over time—comes from the ability to resolve conflict. The ability to face disagreements and to come to reconciliation is the key to whether two people will grow closer or drift apart.

Imagine what a difference it would make in your relationships if you believed that no matter how deep the conflict, you and the person you love had a commitment to work out your differences—that the two of you would simply stay with it until the conflict was resolved. Together you would begin to build a foundation for intimacy unlike any other. You would develop a relationship of trust that would allow each of you to be yourself with the other. That is an amazing gift to give another human being.

Jesus understood how important the commitment to resolve conflict is. He believed that this ability, this willingness to stick to it, is so important that it even affects our relationship with God. In the Gospel of Matthew, Jesus says that our offerings to God should be left at the altar until our conflicts with others have been resolved and we have been reconciled with them (Matt. 5:23-24).

The way to intimacy with another person—resolving conflict—is also the way to intimacy with God. Just as you will have conflicts with those you love, so you also will have conflicts with God who loves you. When that happens, if you simply stay with it—through honest prayer and reflection—

resolution will come, and you will experience the gift of intimacy with God.

Resolving conflict—it is the very stuff of intimacy, of trust, of relationships that last.

Points of Departure

♥ Relationships, friendships between men and women, sexuality: you will be making some major decisions about your life in the years ahead. In the midst of it all, know yourself and your convictions. Don't be afraid to be yourself. Honesty is the only basis on which any genuine relationship can be built.
—From "Significant Others" by Nancy Ferree-Clark

♥ By making and keeping promises to ourselves and others, little by little, our honor becomes greater than our moods.
—From *The Seven Habits of Highly Effective People* by Stephen R. Covey

♥ The communion that can be achieved by human conversation is of great significance for our private lives. . . . It is the spiritual parallel of the physical union by which lovers try to become one.
—From *How to Speak, How to Listen* by Mortimer J. Adler

♥ "It's hard to want to protect someone else, and not be able to," Angel pointed out.

"You can't protect people, kiddo," Wally said. "All you can do is love them."
—From *The Cider House Rules* by John Irving

♥ Falling in love often feels choiceless; it seems to break through our defenses, sometimes even against our will. Being in love, however, is something we say yes to.
—From *The Awakened Heart* by Gerald G. May

Journaling: Ideas for Reflection

Is there someone in your life with whom you feel you can sit down and resolve any conflict that might come up between you? How does the ability—or inability—to do that affect the strength of the relationship?

What are the strengths, the positive characteristics, that you bring to a long-term relationship? What characteristics would you like to bring? How can you work to develop these characteristics?

Prayers: For the World, for Others, for Myself

Give thanks to God for the gift of lifelong love between two people. Pray for those who are in committed relationships, that they may be faithful, trusting, and vulnerable with one another. Pray for yourself as you seek that kind of relationship with someone.

20
&
PAIN, SUFFERING, AND HEALING

Opening Prayer
O God of compassion and mercy, keep all those who suffer close to your heart. Comfort and protect them. Amen.

Scripture Focus
Then they cried to the Lord in their trouble. (Psalm 107:28)

Daily Scripture Readings
Sunday	Isaiah 42:1-9
Monday	Psalm 107
Tuesday	Psalm 23
Wednesday	Romans 8:18-24
Thursday	2 Corinthians 1:3-11
Friday	Isaiah 58:8-9
Saturday	Acts 5:12-16

The Focus for Reflection

I WAS SITTING IN THE CIVIC CENTER IN TALLAHASSEE, FLORIDA. Duke University was playing Florida State in a hard-fought basketball game. Both teams were in the top ten in national polls. The game would be decided on a last-second shot. There were 13,000 fans in the "standing room only" bedlam, but my attention wasn't focused on the game.

Instead, I was watching the broadcasters' bench, where Brent Musburger of ABC television was calling the game and Jim Valvano was doing game analysis.

"Jimmy Vee" was former head coach at North Carolina State University. His 1983 Wolfpack team had won the NCAA basketball championship. I am a graduate of Duke, and since North Carolina State and Duke were arch rivals in basketball, I had often seen Valvano as the "enemy" coach whose team had often beaten Duke.

But today was different. I knew that Jim Valvano had been diagnosed with inoperable cancer of the spine and that he was dying. Across the arena from me sat this courageous man who, in the midst of painful chemotherapy and a terminal diagnosis, was trying to maintain some semblance of normalcy in his life.

As I watched him, I remembered the scene in 1983 when Coach Valvano's Wolfpack had just won the NCAA tournament on a last-second shot. I'll never forget the sight of that man running down the center of the basketball court, his arms outstretched, his eyes and mouth wide open with surprise and jubilation, looking for someone to hug as the celebration began.

Now, ten years later, he was facing a very tough day-to-day struggle. Yet there he was, carrying on with life. When the arena suddenly went quiet during a time-out, I had this sudden urge to stand up and start chanting "Jim-my-Vee, Jim-my-Vee." I wanted to get the whole crowd to chant with me, to let Valvano know that even as his time on earth was coming to an end, he was surrounded by people who were rooting for him, hoping and praying that his struggle could somehow be less painful, less draining.

Jim Valvano died three months later. But during his almost year-long battle with cancer, he had told reporters in interviews of his discovery of the immeasurable value of family, friends, and faith. He said that he had learned, at last, that love was more important than winning, that love would last when victory was nothing more than a memory.

In my mind's eye now, as I remember him, I keep seeing that image of Jimmy Vee running down the court, arms outstretched, surprise and joy all over his face. And, in my mind's eye, I see a figure coming toward Jimmy, with arms outstretched, a joyous face, and exhilaration. Jimmy, at his death, being met by a loving, generous God.

The apostle Paul put it this way: "Where, O death, is your victory? Where, O death, is your sting?" (1 Cor. 15:55) For Jim Valvano, life was to continue, eternal with his Creator.

In the middle of your own struggles with pain and suffering, remember that it is God who created you, God who redeemed you, and God who sustains you, now and forever.

Points of Departure

♥ When the heart is full, the eyes overflow.
—A traditional Jewish saying

♥ [When you are confronted with suffering, you must say]: we are still in God's hands, even in grim situations like this one. This terrible event isn't the last word. And you have to say that with all the strength that is in your being.
—From *God Is New Each Moment*, by Edward Schillebeeckx

♥ As we have seen, there are as many crises, betrayals, and false starts as there are new births and resurrections for those who would follow the desert way of believing.
—From *Soul Making* by Alan W. Jones

♥ The deeper that sorrow carves into your being, the more joy you can contain.
—From *The Prophet* by Kahlil Gibran

♥ If we allow sickness to lead us into wonder about the very base of experience, then our spirituality is strengthened. Accepting that we are wounded, we enter life differently than if our only concern is to overcome the wound.
—From *Care of the Soul* by Thomas Moore

Journaling: Ideas for Reflection

Are you aware of people around you who are suffering physical or emotional pain? How might you help ease their pain?

Reflect on some recent times when you have been in pain. Who was there to comfort you? What did they do to enable you to begin healing?

It's not unusual for someone to feel distant from God in times of crisis. Are you able to stay as close to God when things are going badly as when things are going well?

Prayers: For the World, for Others, for Myself
Make a list of people you know who are in pain. Keep them in your prayers this week. If you are hurting—either physically, emotionally, or spiritually—let God know about it in your prayers. Pray for comfort and strength, both for yourself and for others.

21

&

H U M O R :
Healing the Spirit

Opening Prayer

Lighten my life with laughter and joy, O God. Help me to recognize the daily gifts of humor you send my way. Amen.

Scripture Focus

My heart is steadfast, O God, my heart is steadfast; I will sing and make music. (Psalm 57:7, NIV)

Daily Scripture Readings

Sunday	Matthew 5:1-12
Monday	Psalm 126
Tuesday	John 10:10
Wednesday	Isaiah 55:12-13
Thursday	Job 8:21
Friday	Psalm 30:11-12
Saturday	Isaiah 65:17-25

The Focus for Reflection

WHEN IS A DOG'S TAIL NOT A TAIL? WHEN IT'S A WAGGIN'!

Why didn't God make two Yogi Bears? Because God made a Boo-Boo.

Did you hear about the mummy who went into the bar to have a drink? He just wanted to unwind.

Yes, these jokes are corny—painfully so. Yet they have

a strange power to bring laughter, humorous groans, and a bit of joy.

Medicine, science, and psychology all report significant benefits of laughter to the human body and mind. When we laugh—especially a hearty, deep-felt laugh—our brains release chemicals that can help to relieve stress, anxiety, and depression. A sense of humor is a great gift. Do you have one?

Studies in human relations have shown that the characteristic people most want in a life-partner is a sense of humor. "I want someone who can make me laugh!" We have yet to see any survey of this kind in which having a sense of humor was not one of the top five most desirable personality traits.

Throughout our years serving as pastors, we have found great joy in sharing laughter with people in our congregations and with students in our campus ministries. We have come to realize that as surely as there will be times of stress, sadness, sacrifice, and challenge in our lives, there will also be times for laughter, joy, and celebration.

Seek out laughter in your life. Develop a strong sense of humor. Find a book, a movie, or a group of friends that make you laugh, and visit them often. Whether it's with spiritual companions or the daily comics, settle back and indulge in a bit of hilarity. Your body and your spirit will be all the better for it. And, be assured, God will be laughing along with you.

Points of Departure

♥ Repentance and remorse always come soon enough, but joy can never come too soon.
—From *The Waiting Father* by Helmut Thielicke

♥ God laughs at all the kings and emperors of the earth; the clown makes a joke and reveals that the emperor has no clothes. . . .

A believing Jew or Christian can put this insight into a theological proposition: Redemption will finally be experienced as comic relief on a cosmic scale.
—From *A Rumor of Angels* by Peter Berger

♥ Laughter bursts out of the small world of our seriousness and greed and self-importance and allows the water of life to flow freely to all, relieving the dryness and barrenness of our parched spirits.
—From *The Comic Vision and the Christian Faith* by Conrad Hyers

♥ Celebration is not just a way to make people feel good for a while; it is the way in which faith in the God of life is lived out, through both laughter and tears. Thus celebration goes beyond ritual, custom, and tradition. It is the unceasing affirmation that underneath all the ups and downs of life there flows a solid current of joy.
—From *Lifesigns* by Henri J.M. Nouwen

♥ If you want the gifts of joy and humor in your life, like anything else, you will have to pray for them and work for them every day—day after day.
—From *The Joyful Christ* by Cal Samra

♥ Humor gives us power and a new perspective. It can help us cope and provide the strength to get through the most adverse situations.
—From *The Healing Power of Humor* by Allen Klein

Journaling: Ideas for Reflection
Recollect the funniest thing that ever happened to you. Write about it—what happened, who was there, how you felt, etc.

What's your favorite sitcom on television? What does that program say about you and your sense of humor?

Why do you think God created us with a sense of humor?

Prayers: For the World, for Others, for Myself

As preparation for your prayer time this week, find a book that makes you laugh—a book of jokes, a collection of humor columns, a book of the best cartoons from Gary Larson, Charles Schultz, or *The New Yorker* magazine. Spend a few minutes enjoying your sense of humor as you get ready to pray. Along with your prayers of thanksgiving, petition, and confession, share some laughter with God.

22

🔊
GRATITUDE:
The Power of Giving Thanks

Opening Prayer
Give me a grateful heart, dear God. Keep me mindful of your presence in my life. Amen.

Scripture Focus
Is anything too wonderful for the Lord? (Genesis 18:14)

Daily Scripture Readings
Sunday	1 Chronicles 16:33-34
Monday	Habakkuk 3:17-19
Tuesday	Luke 17:11-19
Wednesday	Psalm 100:3-4
Thursday	Colossians 3:15
Friday	Ephesians 5:20
Saturday	Luke 1:46-55

The Focus for Reflection

IN THE UNITED METHODIST HYMNAL OVER FORTY HYMNS focus on thanksgiving. *Bartlett's Familiar Quotations* and *The Quotable Woman* list almost seventy quotes exploring the meaning of gratitude, with sources that vary from Shakespeare to Hedda Hopper, from Mark Twain to Gwendolyn Brooks. Pick up any Twelve Step program book, and you'll find an emphasis on gratefulness as a crucial element in the recovery process.

From childhood, most of us are taught to say "thank you." From the time I was just beginning to learn to talk, my parents made sure I knew that *thank you* and *please* were the

139

"magic words." And sure enough, as a very young child, I discovered that words of gratitude were, indeed, magic.

By the time I entered first grade, though, I decided I had it all figured out. The words *thank you* weren't magic words after all. Calling them magic was simply my parents' ploy to insure that I would be properly socialized to function in polite society.

Now that I've finished graduate school and I'm well into my fifteenth year as a minister, I've come full circle. I've begun to believe again that words of gratitude are indeed magic words—not magic in the way a child views it, but magic in the sense of allowing me to see my life for what it is: a gift from God.

I've come to see this with the help of many fellow believers, some I know personally and others whom I know only through their writings.

For Henri J. M. Nouwen, a Catholic priest, writer, and spiritual director, gratitude is the spiritual discipline that encourages us to embrace *all* of life as gift—"the good and the bad, the joyful and the painful, the holy and the not so holy." He says that Jesus "calls us to be grateful for every moment that we have lived and to claim our unique journey as God's way to mold our hearts to greater conformity with God's own."

That call—to claim all of life as a gift from God—is sometimes hard for me. Yet, when I surrender to God and offer gratitude, even in the middle of a very tough day, I find myself changed, ever so slightly. I am able to see that life *is* a gift.

In *The Spirituality of Imperfection*, Ernest Kurtz and Katherine Ketcham describe gratitude as a "posture." They compare the posture of gratitude to physical postures. Just as different physical postures allow us to do different things— when we sit down, we can rest or read; when we stand, we can dance; when we lie down, we can go to sleep—so the spiritual posture of gratitude allows us to receive.

On the days I manage to adopt this posture of gratitude, I find that I am able to step out of the way and to let go of the illusion that I can somehow control life. When I do that, I begin to understand just how much *has* been given to me, and I see that a power much greater than I—God—is at work in my life.

Then there's a woman I'll call Joan. She's my mother's lifelong friend, and the two of them have seen each other through all the wonderful things and all the terrible things that have come their way. Joan and my mother seem to have internalized the passage in Ephesians that talks about giving thanks at all times and for everything. They manage to express their gratitude, to God and to one another, no matter what the circumstances. They have shown me the power of gratitude. They know how to accept life graciously, and they understand how gratitude bridges the gap between sorrow and joy.

This week, remember to give thanks. Express gratitude for life as a gift from God, no matter what the circumstances. Say thank you when you feel grateful; say thank you when you don't feel grateful. Allow the power of gratitude to bring you closer to God, to transform your heart, and to move you further along the path of faith.

Points of Departure

♥ Praise and thanksgiving are a discipline. . . . Sometimes this is a natural decision, made without effort because of our overflowing gratitude for a special work of God in our lives. At other times we must struggle to praise God because we feel dry or deprived.
—From "The Heartbeat of Praise and Thanksgiving" by John Koenig

♥ Silence is the proper language of awe and adoration.
—From *Prayer* by George Arthur Buttrick

♥ A miracle is often the willingness to see the common in an uncommon way.
—From *Jacob the Baker* by Noah benShea

♥ Gratitude does not offer thanks only for the good things that happen. It says grace over all the occasions of our lives.
—From "Saying Grace: Living a Life of Gratitude" by Michael E. Williams

♥ [I] end my prayers with the words, "I thank you, God, for all that is good and dear and beautiful." . . .
—From *The Diary of a Young Girl* by Anne Frank

♥ Feelings are fine, but they are also transient and ephemeral; gratitude is not a feeling, but an ongoing vision of thank-full-ness that recognizes the gifts constantly being received.
—From *The Spirituality of Imperfection* by Ernest Kurtz and Katherine Ketcham

Journaling: Ideas for Reflection

Alcoholics Anonymous encourages people in recovery to develop an "attitude of gratitude" as a way to spiritual health. What's the current state of your "attitude of gratitude"? How can you increase your awareness of your life as a gift from God? Are there people you know who approach life from a posture of gratitude? How does it feel to be around them? What can you learn from them that will help you in your faith journey?

Prayers: For the World, for Others, for Myself

Get into the habit this week of giving thanks. Start and end your daily prayer time with words of gratitude and praise to God. Make a special effort to practice gratitude, whether things are going smoothly or not. At first, your practice of gratitude may feel strange, but stick with it. Eventually, the power of gratitude will make itself known.

23
&

FACING CHANGE:
Life in Process

Opening Prayer
Be present in all the changes of my life. Amen.

Scripture Focus
And Jesus increased in wisdom and in years. (Luke 2:52)

Daily Scripture Readings

Sunday	Isaiah 41:10
Monday	Psalm 130:5-8
Tuesday	1 Corinthians 13:7
Wednesday	Philippians 4:13
Thursday	Acts 2:25-28
Friday	Hebrews 11:1-3
Saturday	Job 11:17-19

The Focus for Reflection

"NOTHING ENDURES BUT CHANGE." HERACLITUS SAID IT ABOUT five hundred years before Christ was born. And just because it has become a cliché doesn't make it any less true.

If the statistics cited in an earlier chapter hold, on average you will be moving every five years for the rest of your life. You will also change jobs several times, be in contact with many different kinds of people, and experience the loss of loved ones. Your body will change, your outlook will change, your attitudes toward life will change. Change will, in fact, be a constant part of your life in the years ahead.

Look at the radical changes you've come through just

in the last dozen years. Moving from middle school to high school to college. Leaving old friends and making new ones. Learning to drive, leaving home, voting, becoming more responsible for yourself, gaining independence, managing a budget, being in a close relationship with someone. The watchword over these dozen years is constant—change, welcomed or not, is inevitable.

The "systems theory" out of the social work discipline confirms this. It says that in families, in society, and within individuals themselves, the one thing you can count on to remain constant is change. Nothing, no one, no situation ever stays the same. So a big part of life is learning how to cope with change.

Some changes are easier to cope with than others because they are changes you want to happen. Embracing these changes is natural and easy.

Other changes you face are tougher. Fear and loss accompany these changes, and it's sometimes hard to know how to handle them.

Jesus, in the fifth chapter of Matthew, has a word that can help you through tough changes. "Blessed are those who mourn," he says, "for they will be comforted" (Matt. 5:4). With these words, Jesus calls us to make our way through hard changes by mourning the loss. For if we stick with the process of change, if we surrender to it and mourn those changes that are difficult, the promise is that God will comfort us and help us to move on.

Rely on that promise. When you are faced with hard changes, take a deep breath, put yourself in God's hands, trust God's presence with you through the process of change, and give your sadness and mourning over to God. You will be supported. You will be sustained. You will be comforted. And you will be led along the way.

Remember that you do not have to face change alone—God and the community of faith around you are your constant companions.

Points of Departure

♥ Often it is only in retrospect that we become aware of the mysterious working of God in our lives.
—From "The Weaving and Wedding of Our Lives" by Jean M. Blomquist

♥ "Don't be afraid to learn from fear," said Jacob. "It teaches us what we are frightened of."
—From *Jacob the Baker* by Noah benShea

♥ The idea of change being natural, or even creative, goes against our social conditioning. However obvious and fundamental change may be in our life, our culture and educational system do little to instruct us in how to work through transitions. Because of the upheaval that often accompanies change, we are expected and taught to view change as a calamity. . . . Yet it is possible to accept change and the upsets that may arise out of it as an opportunity to move ahead, to let go of something that is no longer useful for our journey.
—From *The Anatomy of Change* by Richard Strozzi Heckler

♥ Crises and stress themselves are not evil or wrong! What makes the difference . . . is how we deal with crisis and stress.
—From *Avalanche* by W. Brugh Joy

♥ [The] ability to respond gratefully to problems as a learner is one of the first signs of spiritual awakening. At first we just want to stop the pain. But our pain is teaching us something, bringing us somewhere.
—From *Coming to Life* by Polly Berrien Berends

♥ Learning, in fact, is a process of change.
—From *The Anatomy of Change* by Richard Strozzi Heckler

Journaling: Ideas for Reflection

How has your time in college changed you? Have your attitudes and beliefs been challenged or changed? What about your values? What changes in your thinking can you track over the past few months?

What changes are you facing right now? Which ones are you finding easy to embrace? Which are hard?

Can you remember a time when you went through loss because of a change—the death of a loved one, the change in a friendship, some change in your body? Were you able to grieve and mourn that loss? Is there any unfinished business around that loss that you need to continue to work on?

Prayers: For the World, for Others, for Myself
Pray for yourself and for those you know who are facing great changes. Ask for a sense of God's comfort and care amidst the uncertainty. Take time to pray for those people who live in countries facing great political, social, or economic change.

24

&

DOING THE RIGHT THING:
Morality and Ethics

Opening Prayer

Guide me as I seek to follow your way. Amen.

Scripture Focus

Jesus said to [Thomas], "I am the way, and the truth, and the life." (John 14:6)

Daily Scripture Readings

Sunday	Deuteronomy 6:4-9
Monday	Exodus 20:1-17
Tuesday	Mark 4:1-20
Wednesday	Matthew 25:31-46
Thursday	Deuteronomy 5:1-22
Friday	Revelation 3:20-22
Saturday	Luke 6:20-31

The Focus for Reflection

LOVE THE LORD YOUR GOD WITH ALL YOUR HEART, MIND, SOUL, and strength. Do justice. Give food to the hungry and visit the imprisoned.

These commands from the Bible seem straightforward enough. It's a simple matter of morality—knowing the difference between right and wrong, and choosing the right. Jesus wants us to care for those who need care.

Yes, simple enough on paper; but getting down to living your daily life out of that biblical ethic can get confusing sometimes.

There's the often cited example of the woman whose husband is terminally ill. There is one pharmaceutical drug that may cure his disease and save his life, but the drug is still experimental, and the projected market value of the drug is so costly the woman cannot afford to buy it for her husband.

Given the opportunity, should she steal the medication? Should her doctor mislead the insurance company so that it will cover the cost of the drug? Should the government sue the drug's patent owner and seize manufacture of the drug?

No easy answers exist in this dilemma. There are no easy choices to be made. Yet these decisions—like the ones human beings must make every day—are life-and-death decisions.

Balancing competing claims, working through all the implications of your position on an issue, being able to hear the truth in the argument of someone with whom you disagree—this is the stuff of morality. This is what it takes to find ethical consistency—to "do the right thing."

It's not easy, but God calls us to the struggle, and the struggle is worth it.

Points of Departure

♥ Morality is all about how we treat people, including ourselves. . . .

Morality is about doing things to people that result in their rights being respected and their needs being tended to.
—From *Choices: Making Right Decisions in a Complex World* by Lewis B. Smedes

♥ Be patterns, be examples in all countries, places, islands, nations, wherever you come; that your carriage and life may preach among all sorts of people, and to them; then you will

come to walk cheerfully over the world, answering that of God in every one.
—From *The Journal of George Fox*

♥ Only as the love of Christ constrains us to do acts of kindness is our soul changed into his likeness.
—From *The Chain of Kindness* by Paul Tudor Jones

♥ Some of our medicine men always say that one must view the world through the eye in one's heart rather than just trust the eyes in one's head.
—From *Lakota Woman* by Mary Crow Dog and Richard Erdoes

♥ As you live your values, your sense of identity, integrity, control, and inner-directedness will infuse you with both exhilaration and peace. You will define yourself from within, rather than by people's opinions or by comparisons to others. "Wrong" and "right" will have little to do with being found out.
—From *The Seven Habits of Highly Effective People* by Stephen R. Covey

Journaling: Ideas for Reflection

Our assumption is that all of us have made mistakes from which we can learn. Can you think of times when you "went along with the crowd" and, on reflection, realized that wasn't the moral thing to have done?

Racism, sexism, alcohol or drug use, sexuality, personal honesty, and integrity—of all these issues, which do you see the most need to work on in your own life? How will you go about it?

Prayers: For the World, for Others, for Myself
Pray for those who seek to examine their actions under the framework of ethical consistency. Ask God to guide you toward becoming clearer about your values, toward acting kindly in the world, toward treating people morally. In other words, pray that your spiritual growth continues. Pray for those in positions of leadership in this country and around the world. Pray that they maintain integrity and honesty and govern with justice and mercy.

25
𝄢
THE FATIGUE FACTOR

Opening Prayer
Guide me this week, O God, that I may find strength and rest in your Spirit. Amen.

Scripture Focus
In returning and rest you shall be saved; in quietness and in trust shall be your strength. (Isaiah 30:15)

Daily Scripture Readings
Sunday	Leviticus 23:3
Monday	Psalm 4:8
Tuesday	Hebrews 4:9-11
Wednesday	Luke 22:39-44
Thursday	Isaiah 35:1-7
Friday	Psalm 23:1-3
Saturday	Matthew 11:28-30

The Focus for Reflection

IN 1992, NEW YORK-BASED PEPSICO RAN A MARKETING campaign in the Philippines that promised a million pesos (about $40,000) to anyone holding a bottle cap with the winning number on it. When Pepsi announced the winning number, they made a mistake. They announced the wrong number, and instead of having one big winner that night, reports began to flood in from thousands of people over the entire country, all of whom held the winning bottle cap number.

After the error was announced, mobs rioted. Frightened company officials decided at a hastily-called, middle-of-the-night meeting to give anyone with the winning bottle cap number $20 in pesos. That was their second mistake. They thought only a few thousand people had the number. By July 1993, almost 500,000 cap-holders had shown up to claim their money, and reports said that up to 800,000 Filipinos could have the winning number. To top it off, by that same month over 22,000 people had filed civil suits against Pepsi, and more than 5,200 criminal complaints had been lodged.

Reflecting on the middle-of-the-night meeting and its aftermath, one company official said, "You should never make a decision at 3 A.M."

That official may have been referring to what we call "the fatigue factor."

If you have ever lifted weights, run long distances, cross country skiied, or race-walked, you know that it is possible to work a muscle to the point of complete exhaustion. With too much exertion, a muscle can become so fatigued it simply will no longer function. That's the physiological side of fatigue, and it can be devastating.

But fatigue has other facets, too—spiritual, emotional, mental. As surely as you can exhaust your body, you can also exhaust your spirit and your mind. That's why you have to pay attention to the effect fatigue has on you—you literally have to "factor in" the impact of fatigue.

The fatigue factor is universal. The weariness of fatigue can invade anyone's life, regardless of age. Your capacity for overdoing is just as great as anyone else's. Remind yourself often that you are not immune to fatigue, and keep close watch on how you are handling the challenges and pressures in your life.

The fatigue factor is pervasive. If you are emotionally exhausted, the rest of your being—body, spirit, and mind—is affected, too. Stay mindful of that, and don't expect too much of yourself when you are exhausted.

The fatigue factor is insidious. When you are exhausted, your judgment is affected, and you're at high risk of making unwise decisions. If you find yourself exhausted, try not to make any decisions of consequence until you've gotten some rest.

There are two ways to fight the fatigue factor. The first way is to do what Jesus did when he got tired—take some time off. When our Lord found himself overwhelmed, he withdrew by himself to rest and to pray. You must do that, too. When you feel your body getting tired, give it the rest it needs. When your spirit starts to feel weary, feed yourself with quietness, with beauty, and with prayer. When your mind gets overloaded, take a break and go do something physical.

The second way to fight the fatigue factor is to develop habits of rest and leisure that will *prevent* you from getting fatigued in the first place. David Steindl-Rast uses the analogy of the human heart to talk about the importance of doing this. Unlike your stomach muscles, which can only do so many sit-ups before they tire out, your heart muscle keeps working constantly as long as you live. It is able to do that because it has a phase of rest built into each and every beat it makes.

Take a lesson from your heart. Build into your life a rhythm of work and play, exertion and rest. Remember that God rested on the Sabbath, and give yourself room to do the same. Discover what it is that renews and rejuvenates you, and make time to do those things on a regular basis. If you do, you'll find yourself dealing with the fatigue factor far less often.

Points of Departure

♥ Fatigue makes cowards of us all.
—Vincent T. Lombardi

♥ We mess things up by striving too earnestly, obeying too literally, working too scrupulously: we cannot replace grace by effort.
—From *Motherhood and God* by Margaret Hebblethwaite

♥ O Lord God, give peace to us; (for Thou hast given us all things;) the peace of rest, the peace of the Sabbath, which hath no evening.
—From *Confessions* by Saint Augustine

♥ The sun will set without your assistance.
—Jewish proverb

♥ St. John Joseph of the Cross (d. 1734), a Franciscan novice-master, was a cheerful soul who insisted that novices and friars should have a daily schedule of recreation. He recognized that play was important as a balance to worship and work.
—From *The Joyful Christ* by Cal Samra

♥ Stopping work tests our trust: will the world and I fall apart if I stop making things happen for a while? Is life really gifted and the Spirit moving through it, so that I can truly rest and taste this playful caring?
—From *Sabbath Time* by Tilden Edwards

Journaling: Ideas for Reflection

What is your "fatigue factor" like right now? Are you keeping a balance of work and play and rest, or are you on the edge of exhaustion? How can you structure your days and weeks so that you can avoid getting worn out?

What is your reaction to Tilden Edwards' statement that stopping work tests your trust in God? Do you sometimes find yourself working compulsively, either at your class work or in a job? If so, how is your quality of life affected? Do you become irritable, forgetful, short-tempered? Do you know people who are constantly working, who seem unable to stop to rest or to play? What's it like to be around someone like that?

Prayers: For the World, for Others, for Myself

Pray for humility this week—humility to realize that the sun *does* rise and set without your assistance, and that you *can* take time for rest and renewal. If you are exhausted, give that over to God, and ask for help in getting back into balance. Prayerfully examine your work and play habits so that you can be guided to make the adjustments in your schedule that you need to make to stay healthy—physically, emotionally, mentally, and spiritually.

26

&

RACISM:
Color, Creed, and Controversy

Opening Prayer

God, help me to recognize the face of Jesus in the faces of all people and all races. Give me courage to confront racism in the world and in my own heart. Amen.

Scripture Focus

Therefore be imitators of God, as beloved children, and live in love, as Christ loved us. (Ephesians 5:2)

Daily Scripture Readings

Sunday	John 7:24
Monday	Galatians 3:26-29
Tuesday	Amos 5:21-24
Wednesday	John 17:20-23
Thursday	James 3:13-18
Friday	1 John 4:7-11
Saturday	Psalm 67:1-3

The Focus for Reflection

IT WAS AN ESTABLISHED COMMUNITY IN NORTH FLORIDA. When I went there in 1969, it was one of hundreds across the United States struggling with the issue of basic civil rights. The question seemed simple enough—should people in this country be treated equally, regardless of race, color, creed, or religion?

The question seemed simple enough to me. It was my first day in this town and my first day in college. I went into a local restaurant to have lunch and saw a small placard on the top of every napkin holder on every table in the place. It said: "If you are black, we have to serve you. But we don't want your money. Just eat, and leave."

I left that restaurant and never went back again. I told the cashier how wrong I thought the statement was. She laughed at me. I was deeply troubled.

I'm still deeply troubled, because even though there aren't signs like that one in restaurants around the country today, there are still many, many other signs of continuing racism and prejudice. Some of them are subtle; others reek of violence and hate.

The Christian faith says that Jesus calls us to a love that stands against prejudice like this, a faith that calls us to speak out and to act against that kind of discrimination. Sometimes the call to speak and act is loud and clear, and we follow it without hesitation. Other times, prejudice is so ingrained, so hidden, so cunning that we are surprised to find it in our own hearts. The process of ferreting out *this* kind of prejudice is painful, but the gospel call is just as clear—we must give up our prejudice, repent, and turn our lives to "live in love."

The call to fight racism—in others and in ourselves—is a lifelong call and can often be a hard journey. But it is a journey we make in the company of other believers with the guidance of a loving, forgiving God. Commit yourself to the cause of justice and fairness, and God will honor that commitment.

Points of Departure

♥ Hate destroys not only the victim of hate, it also destroys the hater. The first victim of the hater is himself or herself.
—Elie Wiesel, in a conversation with Thomas J. Billitteri

♥ Where racism is practiced, it damages the whole community, not just the victim group.
—From *Black Like Me* by John Howard Griffin

♥ [Racism is] all about failure to recognize the face of God in other people.
—From "The Anti-Racism Primer" by M. Garlinda Burton

♥ When you are tempted to remain silent in the face of racism, stop and speak out of your faith.
—From "Silence Is Assent: Christians and Campus Racism" by Floyd Thompkins, Jr.

♥ Hospitality means we take people into the space that is our lives and our minds and our hearts and our work and our efforts. Hospitality is the way we come out of ourselves. It is the first step toward dismantling the barriers of the world. Hospitality is the way we turn a prejudiced world around, one heart at a time.
—From *Wisdom Distilled from the Daily* by Joan D. Chittister

Journaling: Ideas for Reflection
As you look at your community, what signs of racism—overt and covert—do you see?

How can a person move from judging and reacting to someone based on the color of his or her skin to judging and reacting to persons based on quality of their character?

What do you believe are the reasons for the racial tensions in our society? How do you believe Jesus would react to your list of reasons?

Prayers: For the World, for Others, for Myself
Pray for dialogue and understanding among people of different races, that prejudice and bigotry may be overcome. Remember in prayer the places in your city, the country, and around the world where racism continues to destroy and kill. Search your own heart to find the hidden pockets of prejudice that remain within you.

27

&

CONFESSION:
Bridging the Gap

Opening Prayer

Help me to be honest with you, with myself, and with others, gracious God. Amen.

Scripture Focus

Therefore confess your sins to one another, and pray for one another, so that you may be healed. (James 5:16)

Daily Scripture Readings

Sunday	Psalm 25:16-18
Monday	1 John 1:5-10
Tuesday	Jeremiah 31:31-34
Wednesday	Joel 2:12-13
Thursday	Jonah 3
Friday	Hosea 14:1-7
Saturday	Psalm 69:5

The Focus for Reflection

"YOU'D BETTER CONFESS NOW. YOU DON'T WANT ME TO HAVE to hear from somebody else what you've done. 'Cause if I hear it from someone else, you're gonna wish you'd told me the truth when I asked you."

That was my mother, confronting me and my two brothers when she knew--just by looking at our faces—that we were guilty of some childhood misbehavior.

My mother subscribed to the old adage that confession is good for the soul. At the time, as a ten-year-old, I was quite sure she was wrong. How could confession be good if, when I

169

did confess to something I'd done, I got sent to my room without supper? Confession might have been good for my soul, but I quickly figured out that it wasn't so good for my taste buds or my body.

Years later, as I became familiar with the Twelve Step recovery process, I heard echoes of my mother's adage in the program. More specifically, I heard it stated in the Fifth Step: "Admitted to God, to ourselves and to another human being the exact nature of our wrongs."

I'll admit it. That struck me, on first hearing, as an extreme measure. It was bad enough to face up to my own shortcomings, but to have to confess all that to God *and* to another human being? It seemed a bit much. After all, I rationalized, God already knew all my wrongs, and what human being would still want to associate with me after hearing "the exact nature" of what I'd done?

Then I came across Frederick Buechner's definition of confession, and some pieces began to fall into place. No, confessing your sins isn't telling God anything God doesn't already know; but, he added, "Until you confess them . . . they are the abyss between you. When you confess them, they become the bridge."

That idea was intriguing to me. Those things that most separate me from God could, by my confession of them, be changed into a bridge between us.

That was it—the key to confession and to why it is good for the soul. The great chasm of sin is crossed by the bridge of confession and forgiveness.

Not only is the chasm between me and God bridged by confession, the chasm between me and other people is also covered by that bridge. To say, "I'm sorry; please forgive me" to another person, and to have that person forgive me, is to close the gap between us.

Take a risk. Practice confession—between you and God, between you and other people. It is the bridge that spans the chasms of hurt, pain, and wrongdoing. It is the bridge that leads to peace.

Points of Departure

♥ By contrition we are made clean, by compassion we are made ready, and by true longing toward God we are made worthy.
—From *Revelations of Divine Love* by Juliana of Norwich

♥ The first word in Jesus' ministry was the word *repent* (Matthew 4:17). Repent means not only to confess and be sorry for your sins but also, and more importantly, to turn around. . . . We will not find God until we know we need God.
—From *Becoming Disciples Through Bible Study* by Julia and Richard Wilke

♥ Repentance is a turn in direction that leads to *doing better*. But repentance is also a form of inner healing. Repentance purifies and reroots a soul.
—From *What's So Bad About Guilt?* by Harlan J. Wechsler

♥ There is a difference between recalling one's mistakes and obsessively ruminating about them. . . . This is the sole purpose of remembering what one has done wrong: to avoid repeating mistakes. Making amends wherever possible is reponsible behavior and the only decent thing one can do, but brooding over past mistakes does not accomplish anything for anyone.
—From *I'd Like to Call for Help, but I Don't Know the Number* by Abraham J. Twerski

♥ Private prayer allows us the time—that precious commodity that we say we cannot take—to think about ourselves and know ourselves better. . . . to turn over the stones in our souls and see what lives under them.
—From *To Dance with God* by Gertrud Mueller Nelson

Journaling: Ideas for Reflection

Take some private time this week to examine yourself. "Turn over the stones" in your soul and see what you find. As you do this, remember to be gentle with yourself. Confession is not meant to be heavy-handed and punitive but to be a form of release and healing. Rather than make a list of your confessions, write what it feels like to confess and to be forgiven.

Prayers: For the World, for Others, for Myself

Consider prayerfully this week God's call to confession. Are there confessions you want to make to God, or to other people, that could bridge chasms in your relationship with God, or with others?

28
&

HELP WANTED!:
Asking for What You Need

Opening Prayer

Give me, O God, the wisdom to understand that I cannot do everything on my own. Grant me the humility to ask for help when I need it. Amen.

Scripture Focus

Ask, and it will be given you; search, and you will find; knock, and the door will be opened for you. (Matthew 7:7)

Daily Scripture Readings

Sunday	Psalm 33:20-22
Monday	Proverbs 12:15
Tuesday	Acts 8:29-31
Wednesday	Psalm 46:1-3
Thursday	Hebrews 4:16
Friday	Isaiah 41:6
Saturday	Matthew 7:7-11

The Focus for Reflection

IN AFRICA, AS IN OTHER COUNTRIES AROUND THE WORLD, parables are sometimes told to settle village disputes. James Olá, chief arbiter in the small farming community of Aiyégúnlè in Nigeria, often uses this well-known story about two friends to make a point.

One of the friends was named Anìkàndágbón or "He Who Meets Problems Alone." The other was called Afogbón-ológbón-sogbón or "He Who Seeks Good Advice."

175

The *oba*, or leader, of the town in which these two friends lived had died, and the *oba*'s son took over. As the new *oba* was choosing his chiefs, he heard of the two friends, and decided to put them to a test to see which was the best way to solve a problem. He called them together, put the same test before them, and gave them a week to solve it.

"He Who Seeks Good Advice" went home and immediately asked the entire household to come and help him solve the problem the *oba* had given him.

"He Who Meets Problems Alone" went to his home, and when his relatives asked him about the problem, he sent them away. He told them that he could make decisions alone and that all the knowledge he needed was within himself. He did not discuss the matter with anyone, but sat the entire week trying to solve the problem alone.

At the end of the week, the two appeared before the *oba*. "He Who Meets Problems Alone" had been unable to meet the *oba*'s challenge, but "He Who Seeks Good Advice" had a solution. The *oba* asked the second man how he had solved the problem. "He Who Seeks Good Advice" answered that he had asked people for help, they had made suggestions, he had followed their suggestions, and together they had solved the problem.

The *oba* proclaimed "He Who Seeks Good Advice" the new chief, saying, "He is useful to the community because he solves his problems collectively." The other man, "He Who Meets Problems Alone," he declared a "scourge on the town" and called him selfish because his arrogance had kept him from asking advice and therefore from solving the problem.

The story ends with this moral: "To seek out good advice is best. To try to solve problems by oneself is not good."

It's a straightforward story with a simple moral. But we do not always follow such counsel. Sometimes our arrogance, insecurity, or fear get in the way.

Yet time and again the Bible points to people who

recognized their need for help, asked for help, and got it. Jesus himself asked for help from God in prayer (Matt. 26:39, 42). In Acts there is the story of the Ethiopian who asked Philip to help him understand the writing of the prophet Isaiah (Acts 8:29-31). Nicodemus asked Jesus for help in understanding Jesus' teachings (John 3:1-10). In writings about the early church, stories witnessing to the help Christians gave one another abound.

Don't be afraid to ask for help—from another student, a professor, your campus minister, family members, other people whom you trust. You will face times of loneliness. When you do, ask for help. You will come up against problems that you can't solve on your own. When you do, ask for help. You will have questions about the faith that you can't answer yourself. When you do, ask for help.

Remember: "To try to solve problems by oneself is not good."

Points of Departure

♥ The key to success is active learning on your part. Ask questions, participate in discussions, seek out the professor before or after class or during office hours. There is no such thing as a dumb question.
—From "Don't Know Much About History?" by John Belohlavek

♥ I used to think depending on others was a weakness.
Depending on others became a strength.
—From *Plain and Simple* by Sue Bender

♥ Whenever you need help, ASK QUESTIONS. Never assume that you can learn everything on your own!
—From *Off to College!* by Bob Lowdermilk and Janet Comperry

♥ Sometimes we need to *extend our family beyond bloodlines....* If you do not have anyone in your family who can give you needed encouragement, be reassured that there are individuals who if they know about your plight will offer their special resources, insights, and ideas.
—From *A Gift of Hope* by Robert L. Veninga

♥ [Jesus] carried out his ministry within the context of a small, intimate, covenant community. . . . Why did he do this? He did it because he felt the need to relate to an intimate community whom he could count on being there when the going got tough.
—From *Leading the Congregation* by Norman Shawchuck and Roger Heuser

---

Journaling: Ideas for Reflection
Are there situations or problems in your life where you need help, but you resist asking for it? Spend some time reflecting on what those might be. Ask yourself about the source of the resistance. Is the resistance helpful or not? If it's not helpful, try to find your way through the resistance to get the help you need.

Are there people in your life for whom you could be a help? How can you make yourself more accessible to others, more open and approachable?

When you face a problem you cannot solve on your own, where do you turn for help? Make a list of people you can count on, so that when you do need help, you know who to ask for it.

Prayers: For the World, for Others, for Myself
Pray for the self-knowledge and self-acceptance that allow you to ask for help when you need it. Ask God to show you places where you can be a help to others. Pray for all those who need help, but who are afraid to ask for it.

29

&

VIOLENCE:
When Will We Ever Learn?

Opening Prayer

God of peace and truth, dwell within my heart that I may live in peace and work for peace each day. Amen.

Scripture Focus

The wolf shall live with the lamb, the leopard shall lie down with the kid, the calf and the lion and the fatling together, and a little child shall lead them. (Isaiah 11:6)

Daily Scripture Readings

Sunday	Isaiah 54:10
Monday	Lamentations 3:19-24
Tuesday	Matthew 5:9
Wednesday	Isaiah 2:1-5
Thursday	Romans 8:18-27
Friday	Psalm 46
Saturday	Ephesians 2:13-14

The Focus for Reflection

CONFLICTS RAGE AROUND THE WORLD. WARS—BOTH DECLARED and undeclared—claim innocent lives every day. We deplore the violence, but it continues unabated.

The buying and selling of guns in America continues to spiral, with little or no regulation. We bemoan the increased violence.

In a major Florida city, a tourist is abducted while buying a morning paper, driven to a deserted area, splashed with gas, and set on fire—apparently for no reason other than

181

the color of his skin. We keep trying to measure how far racial tolerance has come.

A woman in her late twenties is finally able to start the long, torturous road to healing, trying to work through the cruel sexual abuse that her father forced on her when she was a child. Meanwhile, as late as mid-1993, the North Carolina legislature is finally debating a bill to repeal the "marital-rape exemption" law, a long-standing law that prevents the prosecution of a husband for rape if the victim is his wife.

Television networks are finding they must broadcast warnings about the level of violence their shows contain, even as these shows grow more and more gory. We wonder how television affects us and our children.

Amidst all the violence, the words of Jesus from the Sermon on the Mount haunt us: "Blessed are the peacemakers, for they will be called children of God" (Matt. 5:9). That verse calls us to live in peace, but it also calls us to so much more.

The call of Jesus to be peacemakers means that we must push ourselves to find ways to make and bring peace to the people and places in our world that are ravaged by violence. We must devote our time, our sensitivities, and our talents to the pursuit of peace. To do anything less undermines the heart of the gospel.

And when, in spite of our best efforts, violence grips us and our world again, remember this: God, who created us and our world for peace, will have the last word. Isaiah's vision of peace will, someday, come to pass.

Points of Departure

♥ The waiting heart arrives at the truth of compassion: that we'll survive as a human family only as we're willing, one by one, to become the place of nourishment for our brother and sister. We'll survive as we cease being individuals struggling alone with our pain and become instead a community sharing our suffering in a great and holy act of compassion.
—From *When the Heart Waits* by Sue Monk Kidd

♥ The world is torn by conflicts, by folly, by hatred. Our task is to cleanse, to illumine, to repair.
—From *God in Search of Man* by Abraham Joshua Heschel

♥ If you shout in an argument, it makes you wrong, even when you are right.
—From *For the Time Being* by Sydney J. Harris

♥ When the inner life is ignored, violence erupts in some form or another, whether in physical or mental illness in the individual, or civil unrest within a nation, or war between nations.
—From *God of Surprises* by Gerard W. Hughes

♥ Great Mam seemed untroubled. "In the old days," she said, "whoever spoke the quietest would win the argument."
—From *Homeland and Other Stories* by Barbara Kingsolver

♥ I keep [my ideals], because in spite of everything I still believe that people are really good at heart.
—From *The Diary of a Young Girl* by Anne Frank

♥ Ultimately, we have just one moral duty: to reclaim large areas of peace in ourselves, more and more peace and to reflect it towards others. And the more peace there is in us, the more peace there will be in our troubled world.

—From *An Interrupted Life* by Etty Hillesum

Journaling: Ideas for Reflection

One can easily be overwhelmed by the level of violence in the world. In the face of that, it's important to identify the small, everyday ways in which you can "cleanse, illumine, and repair" the brokenness that you see around you in your own part of the world. In their book *Random Acts of Kindness*, the editors of Conari Press advocate doing simple things to make the world a more peaceful place—a word of kindness, a note of thanks, a gift given for no reason. What other ways can you think of to make life more gentle for those around you?

Take hope from these small acts of peace. Let them encourage you to get involved with groups, political movements, and faith communities that work toward peace on a national or global level.

Prayers: For the World, for Others, for Myself
Make a list of people you know who are suffering from violence—physical, emotional, sexual, political, racial. Lift them up in your prayers. Ask God to show you ways in which you can help to heal some of their pain. Think of one specific place in the world that is particularly troubled right now. Write the name of that place on a piece of paper and carry it in your pocket this week. Whenever you see or touch the paper, say a silent prayer for peace.

30

ಬ

DECISION-MAKING:
Shades of Gray

Opening Prayer

Clear my mind, purify my heart, and gently guide me in all the decisions I make, O God. Amen.

Scripture Focus

O send out your light and your truth; let them lead me. (Psalm 43:3)

Daily Scripture Readings

Sunday	Amos 5:14-15
Monday	Daniel 6:1-11
Tuesday	Joshua 24:14-18
Wednesday	Deuteronomy 30:15-20
Thursday	Luke 13:10-17
Friday	Proverbs 3:5-6
Saturday	Luke 11:33-36

The Focus for Reflection

A GOOD FRIEND OF OURS SERVES IN THE STATE LEGISLATURE. One morning the Sunday school class he attends got involved in a spirited discussion about abortion. The group was trying hard to understand the feelings and positions of the different class members—positions which ran from one end of the spectrum to the other.

The process the class went through was fascinating. At first, the usual "hand grenades" were launched, and the yes-or-no battle lines were drawn: "Abortion is always wrong." "Abortion should be legal no matter what the circumstances."

After that initial foray, though, some people began to talk about real life situations they or others had faced, and the discussion shifted. People began to understand the gravity and the difficulty of making a decision in reality instead of only in theory. Some began to "step around" to the other side of the table in order to understand another Christian's perspective.

This group of faithful Christians came to realize that decisions about abortion, like so many other decisions, are not easily reduced to simple answers. Life is much more complex than that, and being faithful means working hard to understand that complexity.

Our legislator friend had been quiet throughout most of the discussion. When someone asked him why, he said, "I have been listening carefully to the discussion; it's been a good one. Together you raised many of the instances in which abortion is considered justified by different groups in our society. I am struck by all the different choices and positions taken by people here in this room this morning.

"When the issue of abortion came up on the floor of the legislature, I found myself in the position of having to vote one way or another—yes or no, green light or red light. Because of situations similar to the ones you talked about today—because of the shades of gray involved in making choices like this one—I felt I had only one choice to make. I voted 'yes.' It was one of the hardest votes I ever faced, but my respect for the integrity of each person's right to struggle with that tough issue meant that I had to preserve that right by voting 'yes.' "

Tough decisions. They come your way all through life. The important thing to remember is this: through prayer, reflection, and discussion with other Christians, you will move beyond the point of seeing life in yes-or-no terms, and you will be led by God through all the shades of gray to decisions that honor your intentions to be faithful in a complex world.

Points of Departure

♥ All too often, like Jacob [Genesis 32:24-31], we find ourselves struggling in the dark with a problem, not knowing right from wrong and nearly exhausted from our efforts. We must make a decision, but we just don't know which choice is best. We don't know where the truth lies.
—From *Healing Wisdom from the Bible* by James E. Gibson

♥ Discernment is the secret to living a creative and loving lifestyle with people we want to live with and have to work with; it is the key to making good choices when we are walking on paths where no one has posted signs to tell us where to go. But, like everything else, discernment takes practice; it doesn't come easy.
—From *Choices: Making Right Decisions in A Complex World* by Lewis B. Smedes

♥ It's easy to get just enough religion to protect ourselves from God. . . . We like the kind of religion we can measure, because it protects us from more demanding issues.
—From *Parables from the Back Side* by J. Ellsworth Kalas

♥ I learn by going where I have to go.
—From "The Waking" by Theodore Roethke

♥ There is a big difference between having many choices and making a choice. Making a choice—declaring what is essential—creates a framework for a life that eliminates many choices but gives meaning to the things that remain.
—From *Plain and Simple* by Sue Bender

Journaling: Ideas for Reflection

When Ben Franklin needed to make a decision, he would draw a line down the middle of a sheet of paper; then he'd list the pros and cons of deciding either way. Take a social issue—such as national health care for all people. Use Franklin's method of listing pros and cons. See what your lists look like.

Then take a personal issue—such as deciding between two majors, and do the same thing. Is this method of looking at a decision from both sides of the issue helpful, or not? Why?

Søren Kierkegaard, a nineteenth-century Danish theologian, prayed when he had choices to make. In one of his prayers, he confessed to God that the time had come for him to make a choice and he was afraid of making the wrong one. He tells God that, since he can't put off the choice, he will make it and then trust God to forgive him if that choice is wrong. He also asks God to help him make things right afterward. Kierkegaard's understanding of God's grace toward us as we make decisions is powerful. Remember that in your journal and prayer time this week.

Prayers: For the World, for Others, for Myself
What decisions—major and minor—do you face in the next weeks and months? Use your prayer time to lay them out before God. Ask for guidance in making those decisions.

31

ഔ

FAITH AND POLITICS

Opening Prayer

God, help me to be both loving and just in my personal relationships and in my political decisions. Amen.

Scripture Focus

Be wise as serpents and innocent as doves. (Matthew 10:16)

Daily Scripture Readings

Sunday	Deuteronomy 30:6
Monday	Leviticus 23:22
Tuesday	Luke 4:18-19
Wednesday	Isaiah 11:1-5
Thursday	Amos 5:21-24
Friday	Micah 6:6-8
Saturday	Matthew 5:14-16

The Focus for Reflection

IN THE EARLY SUMMER OF 1776, A COMMITTEE WITH THOMAS Jefferson as its main contributor presented to the Continental Congress the document we know as the Declaration of Independence. Many hailed it as a groundbreaking approach to individual rights and the political will.

One of the more famous lines from this great document declared it "self-evident that all men are created equal." But the "men" in this document included only free, property-owning males. Left out of this declaration were slaves, women, and any men who didn't own property.

From our vantage point today, to exclude these people

from the political process would be abhorrent. Yet many faithful people involved in politics over these last two centuries have sought and fought to control what happens in our society by controlling who makes the decisions. Our "founding fathers" clearly were no different.

As you seek to be a participant in our democracy, and as you exercise your Christian faith in that participation, consider these two observations:

1) A Christian faith—even one strong enough to move mountains—that is not based in love is, at bottom, "nothing" (1 Cor. 13:2).

2) A political stance—even one articulated with great power—that fails to have as its foundation justice for all people is, at bottom, nothing more than empty phrases.

Love-based faith and justice-based politics: The interaction of the two is powerful. It demands that we continually be focused on what Julia and Richard Wilke in the *Disciple* Bible Study call "the least, the last, and the lost." Basic levels of food, clothing, shelter, health care, and education—ensuring these for the least among us, the last among us, and the lost among us is the true measure of a society's greatness. Christians know the importance of this teaching—it is scattered throughout the Bible from Genesis to Revelation.

Faith and politics? Yes! Love and justice? Absolutely! This is the only way to peace.

Points of Departure

♥ If sometimes our poor people have had to die of starvation, it is not because God didn't care for them, but because you and I didn't give, were not instruments of life in the hands of God, to give them that bread, to give them that clothing.
—From *The Miracle of Love* by Kathryn Spink

♥ The courage of heroes gives us strength, and their ideals give us vision. But keep in mind that, extraordinary as these men and women may seem, they are still human beings like you and me. They show that within all of us is the potential to become heroes ourselves.
—From "Larger Than Life" by Phil Sudo

♥ *RESISTANCE* IS THE SECRET OF JOY!
—From *Possessing the Secret of Joy* by Alice Walker

♥ I, too, say let us be peaceful; but the only way to do this is first to assure justice.
—From *Black Like Me* by John Howard Griffin

♥ There is plenty of room for everyone in the world, enough money, riches, and beauty for all to share! God has made enough for everyone! Let us all begin then by sharing it fairly.
—From *Tales from the Secret Annex* by Anne Frank

♥ This is our world, though we did not choose it. Though we may not have been responsible for creating these evils "in the land of the living," yet we must assume responsibility for dealing with them.
—From *Silence on Fire* by William H. Shannon

♥ I am resolved to defend the poor and the weak of every race and hue . . . with the last strength of my body and the last suffering of my soul.
—From "I Am Resolved" by W. E. B. DuBois

Journaling: Ideas for Reflection

Reflect on your involvement in the political arena. Are you informed about the issues? Do you make it a point to know what is going on locally, in your state, and in the nation? How does your faith inform your stance on the different political issues that confront you as a voter?

Prayers: For the World, for Others, for Myself
Pray for the leaders and politicians around the state, the nation, and the world. Ask that they be led to govern with love and justice. Pray about your own political commitments. Ask for discernment and wisdom when you participate in the political process. Pray for God's peace in the world.

32

શ

FORGIVENESS

Opening Prayer

Grant me forgiveness even as I seek to forgive others. Amen.

Scripture Focus

Be kind to one another, tenderhearted, forgiving one another, as God in Christ has forgiven you. (Ephesians 4:32)

Daily Scripture Readings

Sunday	Psalm 130:1-4
Monday	Luke 11:4
Tuesday	Psalm 86:1-7
Wednesday	John 8:1-11
Thursday	Mark 11:25-26
Friday	Matthew 18:21-35
Saturday	Colossians 3:12-14

The Focus for Reflection

"FORGET AND FORGIVE." SHAKESPEARE SAID IT IN *KING LEAR.* Miguel de Cervantes echoed the advice in *Don Quixote.* Alexander Pope, an eighteenth century writer, recognized the importance of forgiveness in "An Essay on Criticism." Dolores Huerta, who worked with the United Farm Workers in leading the grape boycott of the 1970's, talked about the power of forgiveness when reporters interviewed her about her work.

Poets, playwrights, authors, and activists—these and so many others throughout history have struggled with the challenge of forgiveness. It is a fundamental requirement

Jesus himself often taught his listeners, and urged upon them.

And yet, forgiveness remains a difficult task. After years of counseling with adults of all ages, I find that the ability to accept forgiveness for one's self is often a tough hurdle in the healing process.

Time and again, I discover people who cannot—will not—believe that the love of God in Christ reaches out to them across the centuries to accept them, just the way they are. Those who are unable to accept Christ's forgiveness by refusing to forgive themselves effectively close the door between themselves and Christ. But Christ is persistent. He keeps offering forgiveness and the chance to accept it, again and again.

You may be having trouble forgiving yourself for something right now. Imagine that Jesus is standing at your door, wanting to love you in ways that will bring you forgiveness and newness of life. The door, however, has no outside handle. It can only be opened by you—from the inside. You have the choice to open the door, accept Christ's forgiveness, and be loved by Christ, just as you are.

The inability to accept God's loving forgiveness through Christ means missed opportunities to become a new creature in Christ, to change and be changed. Welcome the love of Christ into your life. By offering forgiveness, God has cleared all the obstacles out of the way. Open the door, and meet God on the cleared path by accepting that forgiveness for yourself. Then, seek to forgive others as you have been forgiven.

Points of Departure

♥ Do not be discouraged at your faults; bear with yourself in correcting them, as you would with your neighbor.
—François Fénelon

♥ Forgiveness, then, exerts the most formidable power of all when it enables change. Forgiveness changes circumstances every bit as tangibly as sin does. An act of pardon is just as real an event as an act of sin.
—From *Learning to Forgive* by Doris Donnelly

♥ If you believe your sins are too great for God to forgive, then your God is too small! The true, living God of the Bible offers grace upon grace upon grace, and [God's] grace is greater than *all* our sins!
—From *A Forgiving God in an Unforgiving World* by Ron Lee Davis with James D. Denney

♥ If we did not have to forgive people, we would have no way of manifesting God's forgiveness toward us.
—From *The Heart of the World* by Thomas Keating

♥ [Another] reason to forgive is that in many cases the wrongdoer desperately needs to be forgiven. Even very small misdemeanours can weigh on a person's conscience, and the words "Never mind, I forgive you" can bring great relief.
—From *Forgiveness—The Way of Peace* by Richard Rice-Oxley

Journaling: Ideas for Reflection
In the Gospel of Matthew, after Jesus teaches his disciples what we have come to know as the Lord's Prayer, he comments on only one section of the prayer. Do you know what that is? Look up Matthew 6:14-15 to find out. Why do you suppose he focused on that section?

Sometimes that which we find most difficult to forgive in others are in fact the very things we have done, or do, ourselves. What things are the most difficult for you to forgive in others? As you look at your list, do any of these behaviors or attitudes apply to you?

In Twelve Step recovery programs, the Eighth Step tells followers to make a list of all persons they have harmed and to become willing to make amends to them all. Make your own list of people you need to ask for forgiveness, for whatever reason. Alongside this, make a list of people you need to forgive.

Prayers: For the World, for Others, for Myself
Use your two lists—those people whose forgiveness you need and those people you need to forgive—in your prayer time this week. See if you are led to any action, any "amends-making" with people on your lists.

33

ა

SEXUALITY:
God's Good Gift

Opening Prayer

Thank you, God, for the gift of sexuality. Guide me as I seek to honor this gift. Amen.

Scripture Focus

Or do you not know that your body is a temple of the Holy Spirit within you, which you have from God, and that you are not your own? For you were bought with a price, therefore glorify God in your body. (1 Corinthians 6:19-20)

Daily Scripture Readings

Sunday	Romans 12:1-2
Monday	Psalm 139:13-15
Tuesday	Song of Solomon 7:10-13
Wednesday	Luke 12:23
Thursday	Genesis 2:18-25
Friday	1 Corinthians 10:23-24
Saturday	1 Thessalonians 5:23-24

The Focus for Reflection

IT'S A CURIOUS THING. IF YOU DO NOT THINK ABOUT AND MAKE plans for yourself, someone else certainly will. If you don't make decisions for yourself, there are plenty of others who are more than willing to make decisions for you.

In some areas of your life that might not be so bad. But what we're talking about here is sexuality—*your* sexuality. Not your friends' sexuality. Not your roommate's. Not your parents'. Not your minister's. *Your* sexuality.

205

Sexuality is a tremendous gift from God to you. It is a gift that has the power to draw two people closer to each other in a wondrous intimacy that links the two for life. It can be a source of pleasure, joy, and even new life.

But sexuality can also be a source of pain, hurt, and abuse.

Do you know that some of your peers in college were so sexually abused in childhood that their sense of self-worth has been eroded to a dangerously low level, severely damaging their ability to be physically affectionate?

Do you know that some of your peers are confused about their sexual orientation, paralyzed by shame, fear, and guilt, unsure of who they are sexually?

Do you know that others are so rigidly close-minded about their sexuality that their best approach to this gift from God is to label it "evil" and "sinful"?

Do you know that many refuse to take responsibility for their sexuality by engaging in unprotected sexual activity, putting health and life at risk?

Do you know that there are some who believe the only way to express love for someone is to become sexually involved?

Do you know that there are people whom you respect as professors, whose own sexuality is so confused they may take advantage of your trust in order to exploit you sexually?

Sexuality. A source of joy and a source of pain. Your sexuality is such a precious gift that you must use much care, sensitivity, and discernment as you make decisions about how to live out your sexual life.

And, though these are decisions you must make for yourself, they are not decisions you must make *by* yourself. Trusted friends, other believers in your faith community, words of guidance from scripture—these, along with prayer and reflection, will help lead you to decisions that affirm your sexuality as the gift it was intended by God to be . . . a gift based in love, expressed in long-term commitment, and grounded in respect, awe, and wonder.

Points of Departure

♥ The way you feel about and express your sexuality has an impact on all the other dimensions of your wholeness, for better or for worse.
—From *Well Being* by Howard Clinebell

♥ In the Western world, where everything from blue jeans to bifocals are sold with sex, it is extremely difficult to know how we actually feel about our sexuality.
—From *Centering and the Art of Intimacy* by Gay Hendricks and Kathlyn Hendricks

♥ The Bible in its history treats sexual love with realistic understanding, and in its poetry with power and beauty.
—From *This Is My God* by Herman Wouk

♥ In a culture in which sex has become a consuming issue, a national passion, an underlying current in every social stream, Benedictine spirituality calls for love in breadth and love in depth and love in human, rather than simply sexual, terms.
—From *Wisdom Distilled from the Daily* by Joan D. Chittister

♥ I learned that I, at any rate, could not make love where there was no love. . . . I learned that much that masquerades as love is undisciplined lust.
—From *Two-Part Invention: The Story of a Marriage* by Madeleine L' Engle

Journaling: Ideas for Reflection

You no doubt have heard many opinions from many different people about you, your body, and your behavior. What has been the most helpful advice you've heard?

It's important to think through what you might do if you find yourself in a dangerous, unwanted, or threatening sexual encounter. What would you do? Who would you call? Where would you go? How can you minimize your risks of getting into these kinds of situations?

Prayers: For the World, for Others, for Myself
    Thank God for the gift of sexuality, and ask for guidance in the use of that gift. Pray for women and men who have been sexually exploited, hurt, or traumatized. Pray for courage for the time when you may be able to help someone who has been sexually abused.

34

&

IMAGES OF GOD:
Exploring the Mystery

Opening Prayer

God of many forms and faces, come and dwell with me that I may grow in your Spirit. Amen.

Scripture Focus

My soul thirsts for God, for the living God. When shall I come and behold the face of God? (Psalm 42:2)

Daily Scripture Readings

Sunday	Exodus 17:15
Monday	2 Samuel 22:1-2
Tuesday	Psalm 131
Wednesday	Luke 15:8-10
Thursday	Isaiah 64:8
Friday	Matthew 23:37
Saturday	2 Corinthians 3:17

The Focus for Reflection

JUST FOR A MOMENT, SUSPEND WHAT YOU KNOW—OR WHAT you think you know—about God. Create in your imagination the face of someone you count as a friend. Someone in your life who has ventured past a superficial hello. Someone who knows the signs of sheer joy—or deep pain—on your face. Someone whose powerful caring can pull you from despair to hope, from disillusionment to belief, from pain to healing.

Friends—powerfully present in our lives. But go one step further. Imagine. Just imagine for a moment what it might mean to use the word "friend" to name God.

"Friend." Not Father, or Lord, or King, or Sovereign. But "Friend." Companion.

Imagine it. God—no longer the all-knowing Parent stepping down from heaven to rescue the bumbling child. Instead, God as your Friend, your closest support. Not stepping down, but standing alongside, struggling with you in your pain and rejoicing with you in your joy.

Imagine it. The shift is tremendous. The stress is no longer on what God does *for* us, but rather on what God does *with* us. As Dietrich Bonhoeffer says, to image God in a new way means that we have come of age, we have become adults, and God's new relationship with us calls us to realize, claim, and act on the fact that our decisions—and not just God's will—impact much of what happens in our world.

We are called, by God's friendship with us, to a life of friendship and faithfulness to God, to each other, and to our wider world. It is a tremendous step, to imagine God in this way.

Who first introduced you to God? Carroll Saussy, author of *God Images and Self Esteem,* asked that question to senior high school students in a church-related school. The students were caught off guard—they weren't used to thinking about God from the perspective of the early beginnings of their lives. Some tried to retrieve memories of a conversation with their parents about God. Others tried to recall a time when they first became aware of a "supreme being." Most agreed that their first image of God was of an old man with a white beard on a throne—and many realized that this childhood image of God had not changed, even though they had grown far beyond childhood.

As J. B. Phillips says in *Your God Is Too Small,* it is impossible for people to worship and honor a conception of God that exists in the mind of a Sunday-school age child, unless they are prepared to deny their own years of experience in life. Instead, Phillips and others insist, one's concept of God must change and grow, continually. God is so great, Phillips says, that "We can never have too big a conception of God."

And the sources for re-imagining God? They are limitless—the Bible is full of lively, challenging, provocative images for God. Our own experience, and the faith experiences of others, are rich sources. The long tradition of the church, with its saints and mystics and sinners, provides countless opportunities for reflection. Even science and knowledge, at times considered "enemies" of the faith, reveal new images and understandings of our mysterious God.

Explore. Use your heart, your mind, and your soul. Allow new images of God—as a steadfast rock, a protective mother, a woman searching for her lost coin, a shepherd keeping his flock, a feathered bird offering shelter beneath its wings—to stretch your imagination and deepen your faith.

Points of Departure

♥ Our images of God are critically important to our spiritual well-being.
—From *Recovery from Distorted Images of God* by Dale Ryan and Juanita Ryan

♥ God is an earthquake, not an uncle.
—Yiddish proverb

♥ If we are God's children it might be helpful to imagine ourselves sometimes as in her womb. There could not be a closer image of warmth, security and protection.
—From *Motherhood and God* by Margaret Hebblethwaite

♥ If we *stay open* to letting God be whatever God is, some part of ourselves learns to surrender in love to this God—whether body, mind, or spirit—and thus mystical union begins.
—From *Radical Love: An Approach to Sexual Spirituality* by Dody H. Donnelly

♥ At the center of the Christian faith is the conviction in the universe there is a God of power who is able to do exceedingly abundant things in nature and in history. . . .
    Beyond this, I can only say that there is and always will be a penumbra of mystery surrounding God.
—From *Strength to Love* by Martin Luther King, Jr.

♥ God . . . is both our wings and the wind that bears them up.
—From *When the Heart Waits* by Sue Monk Kidd

♥ God is new each day.
—From *God Is New Each Moment* by Edward Schillebeeckx

Journaling: Ideas for Reflection

Use adjectives to describe your idea of what God is like. What images of God emerge from these adjectives?

How have different artists' renditions of God and Jesus affected your image of who God is?

When you pray, what names for God do you most often use? From your reading of this week's Bible passages, what new or unfamiliar images of God did you discover?

If God is, as some theologians have said, "without form or substance," what implications does this have for you as you try to image God?

Prayers: For the World, for Others, for Myself

Experiment with different images or names for God in your prayer time this week. Take an image that you don't normally use in your prayers—such as Rock or Friend—and use that image as you pray. Let God speak to you in a new way this week.

35
&
HEALING THE EARTH

Opening Prayer
Keep me mindful of your creation, God, and help me
to walk lovingly on the earth. Amen.

Scripture Focus
Make a joyful noise to God, all the earth. (Psalm 66:1)

Daily Scripture Readings
Sunday	Ezekiel 17:22-24
Monday	Genesis 1:1-25
Tuesday	Leviticus 19:9-10
Wednesday	Job 38:4-12
Thursday	Matthew 13:31-32
Friday	Psalm 65:9-13
Saturday	Genesis 9:8-17

The Focus for Reflection

OUR VACATION HOME IN NORTH GEORGIA IS SET ON THE TOP of
a mountain with a majestic lake below on one side and
stretches of mountain ridges reaching out on the other.

When we're able to leave our work at the church and
the hospital for a few days, we go away to this mountain
retreat for rest and renewal. The joke we like to tell about our
time there is this: We sit on the front porch in the morning
watching the lake. At noon, we come inside for lunch, and at
sunset we move our rockers to the back porch to greet the
stars and call it a day.

While this is not exactly the way we spend our days there, the slowed pace we live on the mountain gives us time to take in the beauty of creation all around us.

That beauty is· stunning: lush green forests that breathe out life-giving oxygen. Lakes that nurture animal life and provide refreshment for the earth. Rivers that give us water to drink and generate power for us to see at night. Cascading waterfalls that stimulate the senses and bring peace to the spirit. The mountains that shout the majesty of creation. Valleys so rich with soil that food for our bodies is their gift. Birds whose natural music makes our spirits soar. Breezes that call to us and move great trees with gentle power. Rains and snows that replenish the earth with moisture. The vast, brilliant-hued atmosphere that provides protection from our sun and makes our world hospitable to living things.

Yet, the forests are threatened. Rivers become polluted. Waterfalls dry up because the natural balance is destroyed. The atmosphere is ravaged by manufactured chemicals and toxins. Animals, fish, and wildlife are slowly crowded into extinction.

The threat to nature is clear, and it confronts us daily. But the beauty of nature sends a clear message, too: God is Creator, creation is a gift, and we must cease destroying this creation and heal the wounds being inflicted on our world before it is too late.

It is true that the wounds are great; it is also true that God is with us in our struggle to heal those wounds. People in your community and around the world are responding daily to God's call to faithful stewardship. Listen daily for your own call to stewardship, and you will hear it. Find the simple, small things you can do every day to heal the earth, and join with others in the larger, more complex efforts that will preserve our planet.

God's creation is vulnerable, but remember: it also has the power and beauty to empower us to protect it.

Points of Departure

♥ To nurture ourselves by adopting a simpler lifestyle is to encounter a graceful and comforting place within ourselves and within the world.
—From *The Woman's Comfort Book* by Jennifer Louden

♥ "To wound the earth," he answered earnestly, "is to wound yourself, and if others wound the earth, they are wounding you."
—From *The Songlines* by Bruce Chatwin

♥ If the universe were revered as God's body, one would be less inclined to use the resources of this earth for selfish or mindless purposes and would be more respectful of how God's body is handed on to future generations.
—From *God Images and Self Esteem* by Carroll Saussy

♥ The deep spiritual and ethical emptiness and dis-ease in us as individuals and in our society are root causes of the ecological and nuclear crises.
—From *Well Being* by Howard Clinebell

♥ In *ecological* terms, spirituality is showing respect for all the kingdoms in the community of life—mineral, vegetable, animal, human, spirit, and angelic.
—From *The Meeting of Science and Spirit* by John White

♥ We are facing a winter of great darkness and great hope on our planet: darkness, because Earth is critically wounded; hope, because we begin to be aware of our responsibility.
—From "Sing to the Lord a New Song" by Susan Mangam

Journaling: Ideas for Reflection

In every community, there are local environmental issues that need attention and action. What issues can you identify in your community? How can you put your time and talents to work on these issues? Is there some special place of service to which God is calling you now?

Examine your own lifestyle. How does the way you live every day wound the earth? How does it heal the earth? What changes can you make in your life that will enable you to live more lovingly with God's creation?

Prayers: For the World, for Others, for Myself
Pray for God's creation. Give thanks for the gifts of nature. Ask forgiveness for the ways humankind has abused the earth. Pray for guidance—for yourself and for scientists, politicians, and leaders around the world—that all of us may redouble our efforts to preserve and honor all creation.

36

&

CAN ANYTHING SEPARATE US FROM THE LOVE OF GOD?

Opening Prayer
Ever-present God, show me the way through all of life, that I may walk with you. Amen.

Scripture Focus
And remember, I am with you always, to the end of the age. (Matthew 28:20)

Daily Scripture Readings

Sunday	Psalm 89:1-2
Monday	Exodus 3:7-8
Tuesday	Psalm 121
Wednesday	Isaiah 49:14-16
Thursday	Romans 8:35-39
Friday	Deuteronomy 4:31
Saturday	2 Corinthians 4:16

The Focus for Reflection

IN MY WORK AS CHAPLAIN AT A SMALL PSYCHIATRIC HOSPITAL, I gather with patients and staff every Sunday morning for worship. In many ways, our worship time is no different from what you might experience in your own church or campus ministry. We sing hymns together, talk about our joys and concerns for the week past and ahead, share in community prayer, and listen to a reading from the Bible.

No different, really—until you look closer and begin to notice the worshipers themselves. Some are severely depressed, in despair, and looking desperately for a reason to live. Others have already attempted suicide once, and survived. Some are in the hospital for help fighting an addiction—to drugs, to alcohol, to food. Still others are rape and incest survivors, struggling to put their lives back together.

So when it comes time in the service for me to stand before them, to read the Word, to share a message from scripture, I often find myself struck silent. What word could there possibly be that would even begin to speak to the pain in these people's eyes?

For a few moments, I stand in the silence and let it envelop me. I remember times of great pain in my own life— the suicide of my younger brother, my young nephew's death in an after-school accident, the lifelong battle my father fought with depression, my own struggle with the addiction to perfection. I remember these times, and then slowly, surely, scripture passages *do* come.

From the writer of a psalm, speaking to God: "Where can I go from your spirit? Or where can I flee from your presence? If I ascend to heaven, you are there; if I make my bed in Sheol, you are there" (Psalm 139:7-8).

From the Gospel of Matthew: "I am with you always, to the end of the age" (Matt. 28:20).

From another psalm: "I lift up my eyes to the hills— from where will my help come? My help comes from the Lord, who made heaven and earth" (Psalm 121:1-2).

From Paul, in his letter to the Romans: "Can anything separate us from the love of Christ? No, in all these things— hardship, distress, peril, sword—in all these things we are more than conquerors through the One who loved us." (See Romans 8:35-37.)

The promises of God, the teachings of Jesus, and words of faith from the Bible have sustained believers for thousands of years—these words come tumbling out over our small community of faith gathered in that hospital. And something wondrous begins to happen.

Each one of us—patient, volunteer, and staff person alike—begins to draw some measure of courage and hope from those words. No, God has not left us. Yes, God does suffer alongside us. No, we are not alone. No matter how we feel, we are never alone.

It is a weekly miracle—glimmers of belief born of God's grace. On those days when some among us cannot feel the truth of the promises, the rest of us pledge to believe it *for* them, until the day comes when they can once again feel it and believe it for themselves.

In your times of pain, suffering, and despair, let the words of Romans or Matthew or the Psalms be your lifeline. And if the time comes when you cannot believe the words, reach out and hang onto the lifeline of the faith community. We will believe them *for* you.

Can anything separate us from the love of God in Christ? No! In the words of a creed from the United Church of Canada, the promise is sure: "In life, in death, in life beyond death, God is with us. We are not alone. Thanks be to God."

Points of Departure

♥ God's love is always there whether or not we can feel it, whether we seem good or bad to ourselves or to others, or whether or not we respond to God.
—From *To Pray and to Love* by Roberta C. Bondi

♥ Hope is not identical with optimism. . . . Hope is humble, it is modest, it is selfless. Unconcerned with the ambiguity of past experience, hope implies process; it is an adventure, a going forward, a confident search.
—From *The Vital Balance* by Karl Menninger

♥ God has not left me alone and will not leave me alone.
—From *The Diary of a Young Girl* by Anne Frank

♥ *Never give up.* Never think life is not worth living. I don't care how hard it gets. An old proverb reminds: "When you get to your wit's end, remember that God lives there."
—From *The Measure of Our Success* by Marian Wright Edelman

♥ I don't believe that God would bring me this far just to leave me.
—From "I Don't Feel No Ways Tired" by Curtis Burrell

♥ That which is Christ-like within us shall be crucified. It shall suffer and be broken. And that which is Christ-like within us shall rise up. It shall love and create.
—From *A Common Prayer* by Michael Leunig

♥ Yes, dear souls, God asks only for your heart.
—From *The Joy of Full Surrender* by Jean-Pierre de Caussade

Journaling: Ideas for Reflection
Recall times when you have "gotten to your wit's end." How has God been there—either in spirit or in the form of other people—to meet you? What did those times feel like?

In many ways, the faith comes down to this: trusting God even—or especially—when you cannot *feel* God's presence. Who can you turn to when you are unable to believe that God is with you? Who can "believe that for you" until you are able to believe it for yourself?

Prayers: For the World, for Others, for Myself

Pray for those who feel abandoned by God—people in hospitals, classmates, members of your own family. Ask that they may begin to feel God's presence through scripture and through other believers. Remember in your prayers those who battle depression, addiction, and other deep wounds of the spirit.

Index of Scripture

PSALMS (con't.)		22:9	Wk11
42:2	Wk34	24:13-14	Wk12
43:3	Wk30	ECCLESIASTES	
46	Wk29	3:1-8	Wk10
46:1-3	Wk28	9:10	Wk17
46:10	Wk 4	SONG OF SOLOMON	
57:7	Wk21	7:10-13	Wk33
65:9-13	Wk35	8:6-7	Wk19
66:1	Wk35	ISAIAH	
67:1-3	Wk26	2:1-5	Wk29
69:5	Wk27	6:1-8	Wk17
71:12	Wk 8	11:1-5	Wk31
84:2	Wk 9	11:6	Wk29
86:1-7	Wk32	14:7	Wk 4
89:1-2	Wk36	30:15	Wk25
100:3-4	Wk22	30:18	Wk12
107	Wk20	35:1-7	Wk25
107:28	Wk20	40:28-31	Wk 9
119:33-40	Wk 2	41:6	Wk28
119:105	Wk 5	41:10	Wk23
121	Wk36	42:1-9	Wk20
121:1-2	Wk36	43:4	Wk15
122	Wk 1	49:14-16	Wk36
126	Wk21	54:10	Wk29
130:1-4	Wk32	55:10-11	Wk 5
130:5-8	Wk23	55:12-13	Wk21
131	Wk34	58:8-9	Wk20
139:1-12	Wk15	64:8	Wk34
139:7-8	Wk36	65:17-25	Wk21
139:13-15	Wk33	JEREMIAH	
143:7-10	Wk16	31:31-34	Wk27
PROVERBS		LAMENTATIONS	
3:5-6	Wk30	3:19-24	Wk29
3:13-26	Wk 2	3:22	Wk16
4:5	Wk 2	EZEKIEL	
11:25	Wk11	17:22-24	Wk35
12:15	Wk28	37:1-14	Wk16
17:1	Wk11	DANIEL	
17:9, 17	Wk18	6:1-11	Wk30
20:6-7	Wk 7		

ACKNOWLEDGMENTS

The publisher gratefully acknowledges permission to reprint excerpts from the following copyrighted material:

Sue Bender: From *Plain and Simple: A Woman's Journey to the Amish.* Copyright © 1991 by Sue Bender. Reprinted by permission of HarperCollins Publishers, Inc.

Joan D. Chittister: From *Wisdom Distilled from the Daily.* Copyright © 1990 by Joan D. Chittister. Reprinted by permission of HarperCollins Publishers, Inc.

Howard Clinebell: From *Well Being.* Copyright © 1992 by Howard Clinebell. Reprinted by permission of HarperCollins, Publishers, Inc.

Stephen R. Covey: From *The Seven Habits of Highly Effective People.* Copyright © 1989 by Stephen R. Covey. Reprinted by permission of Simon & Schuster.

Nancy Ferree-Clark: From "Significant Others" from *Orientation '88.* Copyright © 1988 by the United Methodist Board of Higher Education and Ministry, Nashville, TN. Used by permission.

Richard Strozzi Heckler: From *The Anatomy of Change.* Copyright © 1984 by Richard Strozzi Heckler. Reprinted by arrangement of Shambhala Publications, Inc. 300 Massachusetts Ave. Boston, MA 02115.

Abraham Joshua Heschel: From *God in Search of Man.* Copyright © 1955 by Abraham Joshua Heschel, renewed © 1984 by Sylvia Heschel. Reprinted by permission of Farrar, Straus & Giroux, Inc.

Eva Hoffman: From *Lost in Translation.* Copyright © 1989 by Eva Hoffman. Used by permission of Dutton Signet, a division of Penguin Books USA, Inc. and William Heinemann, Ltd.

ABOUT THE AUTHORS

HELEN R. NEINAST is chaplain and director of pastoral services at Charter Hospital of Pasco County in Florida. She was formerly a director in the Division of Higher Education at the Board of Higher Education and Ministry of The United Methodist Church. She holds the Master of Divinity degree from Duke University Divinity School, and is a clergy member of the New Mexico Conference of The United Methodist Church.

THOMAS C. ETTINGER is pastor of First United Methodist Church in Land 'O Lakes, Florida. He has been a campus minister at Florida Atlantic University and Florida State University, and a mental health counselor in private practice in Tallahassee, Florida. He received the Master of Divinity degree from Duke University Divinity School and is a clergy member of the Florida Conference of The United Methodist Church.

They live in Land 'O Lakes, Florida, with their thirteen-year-old retriever, Puppy, and their three-year-old cat, Elizabeth. They have recently been named United Methodist campus ministers at Emory University in Atlanta, Georgia, effective in June 1994.